CONTENTS

⊗ THIS IS OXFORDSHIRE

⊗ YOUR OXFORDSHIRE STORY

⊗ TRAVEL TOOLKIT

All information stated in this guide is correct at time of publishing and every attempt is made to ensure its accuracy. However, prices, opening hours and offers may be subject to change without notice. Please check before you travel.

WE[L]

Oxf[ord]

"Dear friends,

Oxfordshire is a wonderful place to visit. It is a labyrinth of storied places and people. As a young man in my native France, I knew Oxford from books; I loved its architecture and history, and I dreamed of coming here. I first came here at the age of 22. When I saw the beautiful Oxfordshire villages, cricket on the greens, bobbies on the beat, then the city itself, I fell in love. Now, nearly 50 years later, I can claim to be a local boy. I opened Belmond Le Manoir aux Quat'Saisons in 1984 and 23 years ago created the very first Brasserie Blanc. Oxford is my second home.

Here you will find so many hidden treasures in Oxfordshire; the city's university buildings and museums, the traditional market towns and some of the most beautiful Cotswold villages. Oxfordshire is a place steeped in history and heritage. It is home to famous literary figures and unique traditions, there is so much richness for you to explore.

WELCOME TO Oxfordshire

With skylines pierced with spires and domes, palace estates and idyllic meadows, the entire county has a dreamlike quality. I love to feed my imagination by strolling alongside the River Thames, or across Oxfordshire's rolling hills. Tucked away in the countryside, the 15th century manor of Belmond Le Manoir aux Quat'Saisons is my personal place of inspiration; surrounded by lawns, flower borders and orchards, our Oxfordshire setting is postcard-perfect.

I am sure this guide will spark your curiosity and inspiration of all the fantastic places and attractions Oxfordshire has to offer. We very much look forward to welcoming you on your next visit."

Raymond Blanc

**Raymond Blanc OBE,
Chef Patron at Belmond Le
Manoir aux Quat'Saisons**

www.experienceoxfordshire.org

TOP 10 ATTRACTIONS
in Oxfordshire

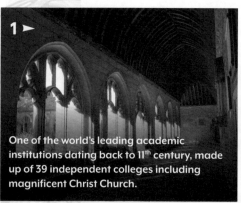

One of the world's leading academic institutions dating back to 11th century, made up of 39 independent colleges including magnificent Christ Church.

Home to the 12th Duke of Marlborough and his family, the birthplace of Sir Winston Churchill and a UNESCO World Heritage site.

Europe's ultimate luxury shopping destination, home to more than 160 world-leading brands, from Swarovski to Saint Laurent; all offering exceptional savings.

1 ► University of Oxford

2 ► Blenheim Palace **♀ C3 County**

3 ► Bicester village **♀ D3 County**

4 ► Ashmolean Museum **♀ C2 City**

5 ► Westgate **♀ C4 City**

6 ► Oxford Castle & Prison **♀ C4 City**

7 ► Cotswold Wildlife Park and Gardens **♀ B4 County**

8 ► Cogges Manor Farm **♀ C4 County**

9 ► Oxford University Museum of Natural History **♀ D1 City**

10 ► The Thames

4 ►

The world's oldest public museum, home to a world-famous collection of art and artefacts ranging from Egyptian mummies to contemporary art.

5 ►

Major retail and lifestyle destination in the centre of Oxford, home to prestigious global brands plus eclectic restuarants and sophisticated rooftop dining.

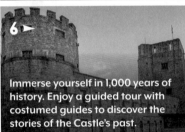

6 ►

Immerse yourself in 1,000 years of history. Enjoy a guided tour with costumed guides to discover the stories of the Castle's past.

7 ►

Home to more than 250 species of animals and 160 acres of beautiful parkland in West Oxfordshire.

8 ►

A 17th century farmstead in the Cotswolds with picnic orchard, farm animals, museum and café. Features as Yew Tree Farm in Downton Abbey.

9 ►

Situated in an impressive neo-Gothic building, the museum offers a variety of different permanent collections and exhibitions, next to quirky sister Pitt Rivers Museum.

10 ►

There is so much to do on the river, from punting and cruises to walks with incredible riverside views.

OXFORD VISITOR INFORMATION CENTRE

Find out what more there is to see and do in Oxfordshire at the Oxford Visitor Information Centre. Pick up leaflets, guide books, gifts, book tickets for attractions or speak to our multilingual team.

📞 01865 686430 🖵 www.experienceoxfordshire.org

Find us:

**15-16
Broad Street,
Oxford,
OX1 3AS**

THE OXFORD PASS

Just £69 for a two day pass,
giving you access to Oxfordshire's
amazing attractions and bus travel

THE OXFORD PASS

Enjoy the best Oxfordshire has to offer with the Oxford Pass;
the city's official sightseeing card.

#OxfordPass
OXFORDPASS.COM
For terms and conditions visit the website

OXFORD VISITOR INFORMATION CENTRE
LEFT LUGGAGE

⊗ **Store your luggage while you explore**

⊗ **Leave your shopping and enjoy lunch**

Open 7 days a week
within shop opening hours

£5 for up to 3 hours
£8 for same day collection
£10 for up to 24 hours

At the Oxford Visitor Information Centre
15 - 16 Broad Street, Oxford, OX1 3AS

www.experienceoxfordshire.org/left-luggage

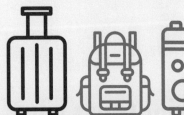

Experience OXFORDSHIRE
experienceoxfordshire.org

OXFORD OFFICIAL WALKING TOURS

- **University and City Tour**
- **C.S. Lewis & J.R.R. Tolkien Tour**
- **Inspector Morse, Lewis & Endeavour Tour**
- **Oxford Pubs Tour**
- **specialist tours available including:**
Harry Potter, Film & TV, Philip
Pullman - see our site for details

All our tours are led by our own friendly and accredited guides.

Tours **include** entrance fees to colleges and other University of Oxford buildings.

As well as running up to 5 scheduled tours per day, all our regular tours (plus many more) can be booked just for your group.

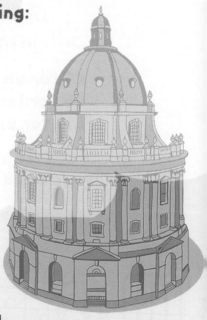

01865 686442
🐦 **@OfficialToursOx**
officialtours@experienceoxfordshire.org
www.oxfordofficialwalkingtours.com

OXFORD
An Introduction

On a trip to **Oxford** be sure to squeeze in a visit to a world-class museum before a picnic in one of the city's tranquil parks. Stroll along Oxford's pastel-hued **High Street** lined with independent boutique shops and coffee bars, before joining the **River Cherwell** at **Magdalen Bridge** for a leisurely punt along the river.

Make sure that you leave time to explore and enjoy the eclectic variety of places to eat and drink the city has to offer, from chic five-star restaurants to buzzing pubs and cafes.

During your visit the friendly, international team at the **Oxford Visitor Information Centre** on **Broad Street** will be happy to answer all your questions.

Take a walking tour of Oxford city centre, where ornate buildings in distinctive golden stone can be found around every corner. The **University of Oxford**, the oldest university in the English-speaking world, is made up of 39 colleges - many date back to medieval times and have immaculate lawned quads, grand dining halls and ornate chapels.

1 ► *Sheldonian Theatre*
2 ► *Balliol College Library*
credit Sarah Rhodes
3 ► *Radcliffe Camera*

OXFORD
City Map

(i) **VISITOR INFORMATION CENTRE
& Oxford Official Walking Tours**
15-16 Broad Street, Oxford, OX1 3AS D3

P CAR PARK

◎ GREAT PHOTO SPOT

100m ⌐ 500ft ⌐ _____ SCALE

☐ **GRID SQUARE = 900ft/275m**

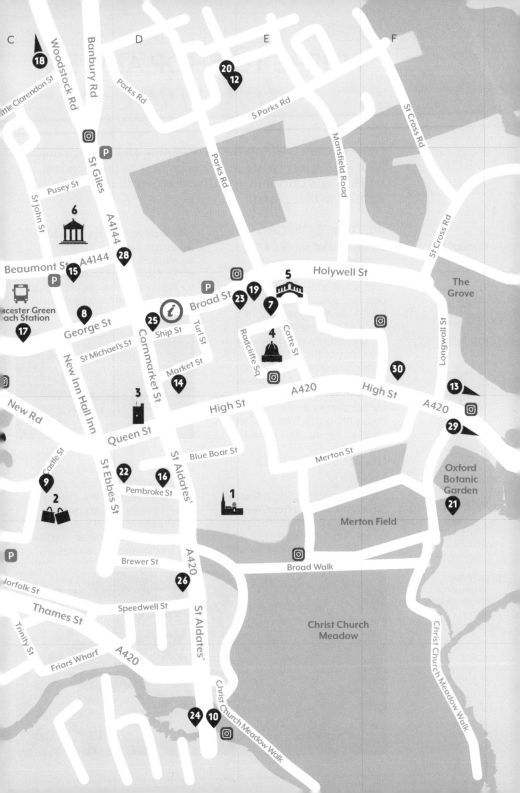

WHERE TO SHOP AND EAT
in Oxford

Oxford is a hub of top-notch shopping and dining choices with high street shops and eateries next to independent retailers and cafes and exclusive designer brands - all waiting to be enjoyed!

Great for

FOOD & DRINKS

CULTURE

HIDDEN GEMS

Build these recommendations into your Oxford itinerary
Read More | p.62 ►

WESTGATE OXFORD

Westgate Oxford (♀ **C4 City**) is home to prestigious global brands, innovative restaurants and cafes, a five-screen cinema and sophisticated boutique bars. Visit **Westgate's** rooftop terrace for arresting views of the **Oxford** city skyline while you enjoy one of the many dining or drinking options! Some of our favourites include **Cinnamon Kitchen**, specialising in innovative contemporary Indian cuisine, **Pho**, with its delicious and healthy Vietnamese-inspired street food,

and **Victors**, offering affordable American luxury in the form of signature small plates and fine wine. You'll love **The Alchemist** for their theatrical cocktails, and **Shoryu Ramen** for authentic Hakata tonkotsu ramen.

GLOUCESTER GREEN MARKET

Located just off bustling **George Street**, the **Gloucester Green Market** is a traditional open-air market that operates from Wednesday through to Saturday.

Here you will find a vibrant selection of fresh and seasonal fruits and vegetables, cheese, baked goods, sweets and more. Don't leave without trying the delicious street food served here, inspired by global cuisines.

OXFORD COVERED MARKET

Home to a collection of independent shops, the **Covered Market** (♥**D3 City**) dates back to the 18th century and is a hub of wonderfully tucked-away retailers selling everything from kitchenware and cakes to hand-crafted gifts, jewellery and male grooming products. Eating here is an experience you won't find anywhere else in the city; watch the skilled bakers of **The Cake Shop** create masterpieces before popping in to buy a cupcake, kick start your day with a full English breakfast at **Browns**, or quench your thirst at a juicery, coffee shop or the rooftop cocktail bar.

Where to Shop and Eat in Oxford

Discover local gems
Read More | p.18 ➤

HIGH STREET

Oxford's picturesque and busy **High Street**, known locally as 'The High', runs from **Carfax Tower** (♥ **D4 City**) all the way down and east to **Magdalen Bridge**. Aside from the multiple colleges lining the way, Oxford's High Street features a plethora of book shops, clothing stores, restaurants and antiques dealers. In addition, Oxford's High Street boasts England's original coffeehouse - one that's been around since the 1650s!

For more ideas, see our listings pages
Read More | p.87 ➤

LITTLE CLARENDON STREET

Buzzing **Little Clarendon Street** has stylish boutiques, cheese shops, vintage retailers, and more. Walk to the end of Little Clarendon Street and you will find yourself in the relaxed and bohemian area of **Jericho**, which boasts more independent shops, bookstores and unique drinking establishments.

OXFORD'S
Green Spaces

Offering leafy sanctuaries from the bustling city, Oxford's green spaces are open to the public all year round. Take some tranquil time out from your city break in these historic parks.

Great for

NATURE LOVERS

FAMILIES

HIDDEN GEMS

PORT MEADOW

One of **Oxford's** hidden gems, **Port Meadow** is a beautiful open area of ancient meadowland, north-west of the city centre and just a 5-minute walk from **Jericho**, offering a tranquil retreat for visitors and locals alike. Home to grazing horses and a herd of pedigree Old English Longhorn cattle, Port Meadow lies alongside the **River Thames** and has provided inspiration for **Lewis** Carroll's *Alice in Wonderland* and JRR Tolkien's *Lord of the Rings*.

CHRIST CHURCH MEADOW

Ideal for short scenic walks and picnics, **Christ Church Meadow** stretches from **Christ Church College** to the banks of the River Thames and **River Cherwell**. The meadow itself is an open expanse of rugged greenery, peppered with rare English Longhorn cows. Walk around the meadow to take in a variety of wildlife, watch the rowing boats passing by on the river, or see the college boathouses.

SOUTH PARK

In **East Oxford**, at the end of **St Clements**, you'll find **South Park**. The largest park in the city, with 50 acres of open green space, South Park often plays host to events and festivals throughout the year. It's the perfect park for dog walks, sun-bathing, and meeting with friends before lunch at one of the many excellent restaurants on **Cowley Road** or St Clements.

South Park also boasts excellent views over the spires of Oxford, especially in the mesmerising light of dawn or dusk.

See more nature along Oxford's waterways
Read More | p.38 ➤

Oxford's Green Spaces

UNIVERSITY PARKS

University Parks offers the perfect escape from the hustle and bustle of the city but is also conveniently located right at the city's heart. The beautiful park, originally created by **Merton College** and now owned by the **University of**

Oxford itself, offers a choice of peaceful walks. Feed ducks at the pond and discover the park's **Genetic Garden** and collection of rare trees before wandering back towards the city centre along the bank of the River Cherwell.

OXFORD BOTANIC GARDEN

The **University of Oxford Botanic Garden** is the UK's oldest botanic garden, founded in 1621 to grow plants for medicinal research. Situated in the heart of Oxford, the historic garden is an oasis of

green in the city centre. Take a stroll around the formal walled garden; see exotic, tropical and carnivorous plants in the glasshouses, and enjoy the lush herbaceous borders of the informal lower garden.

Stretch your legs further with a walk along the Ridgeway Trail
Read More | p.70 ➤

1 ➤ *Port Meadow*
2&3 ➤ *Christ Church Meadow*
4 ➤ *South Park*
5to8 ➤ *Botanic Garden*
(8) credit: Timothy Walker

WHERE THE LOCALS LIVE:
Beyond the City Centre

Travel just beyond Oxford city centre and you will find great attractions and local culture in many of the city's districts - each with their own unique identity.

Great for

ADVENTURERS

CULTURE

HIDDEN GEMS

JERICHO

Once an industrial area due to its proximity to the **Oxford canal, Jericho** is now one of **Oxford's** most sought-after areas to live with an excellent choice of pubs, restaurants and shops. It's a laid-back, bohemian neighbourhood, characterised by hip cocktail bars and quiet residential streets of Victorian terraces. **The Old Bookbinders Ale House** is a charming neighbourhood pub loved by locals for its delicious (and surprising!) menu of French cuisine. For a fun evening, head to **Jericho Tavern** for some live music, or enjoy expertly-mixed cocktails at **Raoul's Bar**.

1 ▶

Discover nearby
green spaces in
the city
Read More | p.16 ➤

SUMMERTOWN

To the north of the city centre, **Summertown** is a leafy suburb that is lined with cosy cafes, boutique shops, and many independent restaurants and eateries. **North Parade** and **South Parade** are colourful shopping streets, perfect for picking up an artisan gift or pastry to take home.

On a Sunday **Summertown Farmers Market** springs to life, offering a tempting array of incredible fresh produce. Experience peace and tranquillity in nearby **Turrill Sculpture Garden**, or find entertainment at the **North Wall Arts Centre**, which showcases upcoming artists across comedy, theatre and dance.

COWLEY ROAD

Cowley Road is a vibrant, multicultural area to the east of Oxford with many restaurants, shops, bars and arts venues. The area's unique character is celebrated every July at the **Cowley Road Carnival**, which boasts live music, a lively parade and delicious street food. One

of the most diverse restaurant scenes in the city, Cowley Road boasts the hottest spots for food shopping and restaurants. The tiny, crammed **Maroc Deli** is a total gem, and just a few yards away is bustling **Arbequina**, masquerading under the name of 'R Neville Chemists', which serves truly exceptional tapas.

Find the
perfect place
to stay in our
accommodation
listings
Read More | p.87 ➤

ST CLEMENTS

Adjacent to Cowley Road, **St Clements** is another street bustling with a variety of eclectic restaurants and bars - the **Oxford Brookes University** campus is nearby, giving the feel of a buzzing student district. Visit lively Sri-

Lankan street food restaurant **The Coconut Tree** or creative cocktail bar **Be At One** to experience the atmosphere! Wander on from St Clements and you will come to **South Park**; a beautiful, vast green space overlooking Oxford's dreaming spires.

19

The Oxfordshire Museum

Woodstock

Oxfordshire's story from dinosaurs to the Anglo-Saxons and Victorians. Special exhibitions.

Free Admission

Opening times:
Tues–Sat: **10am–5pm**
Sun: **2pm–5pm**

Oxfordshire.gov.uk/museums
Park Street, Woodstock, OX20 1SN
🐦 **@oxonmuseum** f **@oxonmuseum**

OXFORDSHIRE COUNTY COUNCIL

OXFORDSHIRE
An Introduction

Walk across the ancient chalk downs of the **Ridgeway** and climb to the top of **White Horse Hill** for enchanting views over the whole of **Oxfordshire**, with its rolling hills dotted with sheep, criss-crossed with hedges and circled by red kites, continuing endlessly into the horizon. Simply relax and take a break as you admire the scenery, but don't stop for too long – for there is so much to see and do on your journey across the county.

Standing in the ancient and unspoilt countryside of the **Chiltern Hills** stretching across the south of Oxfordshire, it feels like you might be the first traveller to discover this land. Venture north through the county, however, and you'll discover thousands of years of culture.

Meandering across the county, the **River Cherwell** and **River Thames** provide beautiful riverside walks. Follow the River Thames north to shop in a farmers' market in one of Oxfordshire's traditional market towns, such as **Wallingford** or **Abingdon**.

The two rivers converge in **Oxford**, an architectural gem and the county (and world)'s intellectual heart. Piercing Oxfordshire's skylines with its spires and domes, the lively city provides an energetic contrast to the tranquillity of Oxfordshire's countryside.

Let the River Cherwell guide you further north through the county, towards the uplands known as 'ironstone country', with pretty villages built of the richly coloured local Hornton ironstone, the market towns of **Banbury** and **Bicester**, plus welcoming pubs and blissfully quiet walking trails.

Head west in the county and you will find that some of the most beautiful **Cotswold** villages, such as **Minster Lovell** and **Burford**, are in Oxfordshire. Relax with an afternoon tea in a charming, honey-coloured Cotswold village.

With a wealth of natural beauty, Oxfordshire is an unmissable county bursting with character. Take some time to explore beyond the city of Oxford, because there is so much more to discover.

1 ➤ *River Cherwell*
2 ➤ *White Horse Hill*

21

CHERWELL
The Impressive North

Great for

ADVENTURERS

NATURE LOVERS

HIDDEN GEMS

1 ► *Bicester Village*
2 ► *The Fine Lady*
3 ► *Hook Norton Brewery*

North Oxfordshire offers rich rewards for its visitors. Centred in the valley of the **River Cherwell**, with the **Oxford Canal** alongside, there are landscapes of beautiful countryside with picturesque villages and the market towns of Banbury and Bicester to explore.

Banbury (📍 **C2 County**) is set amidst the gentle rolling hills in the north of the district. An impressive bronze statue of the "Fine Lady" from the famous 'Ride a cock horse to Banbury Cross' rhyme is set close to the **Banbury Cross** at the meeting point of the roads from **Oxford**, **Warwick** and **Shipston-on-Stour**. Other points of interest include the **Market Place**, the atmospheric lanes of the **Old Town** and the **Castle Quay** shopping mall with the town's **Museum** set directly beside the Oxford Canal.

Bicester (📍 **D3 County**) lies just 12 miles northeast of Oxford and marries the charm of an historic market town with the appeal of the world-famous retail outlet of **Bicester Village** (📍 **D3 County**). Trains from **London Marylebone** to Bicester take only 46 minutes and as well as shopping at the Village you can visit the delightful **Garth Park** gardens and relax over a meal in one of the town's traditional pubs or restaurants which serve Chinese, Thai, Turkish, Indian and Italian cuisine.

The uplands northwest of Banbury are known as 'ironstone country', with pretty villages built of the richly coloured local **Hornton** ironstone, welcoming pubs, and interesting

walking and cycling routes. Well worth a visit is the moated manor house of **Broughton Castle** (📍 **C2 County**), built in the 14th century and used as a film setting for both **Shakespeare in Love** and **The Madness of King George**.

There is a rich brewing heritage to discover in the village of **Hook Norton** (📍 **C2 County**), near **Chipping Norton**, where you can enjoy a tour of the Victorian **Hook Norton Brewery** which is still thriving today and supplying many local pubs.

Built in the late 18th century to carry commercial barges between Coventry and **Oxford**, the Oxford canal follows the scenic course of the River Cherwell. You can explore the canal by hiring narrow boats at either **Lower Heyford** or **Thrupp**, or enjoy one of the towpath or circular walks. The stretch of the canal between Banbury and Oxford is also accessible by train, with stations at **Banbury**, **Lower Heyford**, **Tackley** and **Oxford.**

The district has a strong tradition of festivals and events, ranging from Bicester's summer music events at Garth Park and the motor events at Bicester Heritage to **Banbury's Food Festival** and **Cropredy's Fairport Convention** music festival held in August each year. A central location with excellent transport links, North Oxfordshire is not only a rewarding destination, but also an ideal touring centre. A wide range of overnight accommodation provides ease of access to many world-famous destinations, including **Silverstone Circuit**, **Blenheim Palace**, **Oxford**, **Warwick Castle**, **Stratford-upon-Avon**, and the **Cotswolds**.

Walk along Oxford Canal to explore the heart of the Cherwell valley
Read More | p.66 ►

BICESTER VISITOR CENTRE

Bicester Village Outlet Shopping Centre, Pingle Drive, Bicester, OX26 6WD

📞 **01869 366 266**   🖥 **bicestervisitorcentre@valueretail.com**

BANBURY TOURIST INFORMATION CENTRE

(entrance within Castle Quay)
Banbury Museum, Spiceball Park Road, Banbury, OX16 2PA

📞 **01295 236 165**   🖥 **tourist.information@banburymuseum.org**

1 ► *Oxford Canal*
2 ► *Broughton Castle*

DICOVER A DIFFERENT KIND OF VILLAGE

Bicester Village, home to more than 160 boutiques

Leave the hustle and bustle behind and head to Bicester Village where you'll enjoy up to 60% off the recommended retail price at boutiques from leading brands including Maje, Missoni, Golden Goose and The White Company.

Make a day of it with delicious dining at Café Wolseley, farmshop restaurant & cafe by Soho House & Co or Asian restaurant Shan Shui. Enjoy ample complimentary parking or travel by train with direct journeys from Oxford from just 15 minutes and from London Marylebone from just 46 minutes.

Open seven days a week. For opening hours, please visit **BicesterVillage.com** or download the app.

SOMETHING
EXTRAORDINARY
EVERY DAY

BICESTER
VILLAGE

A MEMBER OF THE BICESTER VILLAGE
SHOPPING COLLECTION®

EUROPE BICESTER VILLAGE **LONDON** | KILDARE VILLAGE **DUBLIN** | LA VALLÉE VILLAGE **PARIS** | WERTHEIM VILLAGE **FRANKFURT**
INGOLSTADT VILLAGE **MUNICH** | MAASMECHELEN VILLAGE **BRUSSELS** | FIDENZA VILLAGE **MILAN** | LA ROCA VILLAGE **BARCELONA**
LAS ROZAS VILLAGE **MADRID** | **CHINA** SUZHOU VILLAGE **SUZHOU** | SHANGHAI VILLAGE **SHANGHAI**

SOUTH OXFORDSHIRE
Hills & Villages

Explore country houses, visit local museums and enjoy the unspoilt landscape of the **Chiltern Hills, River Thames, Berkshire Downs** and the **Ridgeway**.

Relax in charming villages and enjoy the historic market towns with their unique mix of independent retailers and high street shops. Weekly markets showcase the very best produce and artisan wares from talented craftspeople.

Thame (♀ E4 County) is a market town at the foot of the Chiltern Hills, just 14 miles from **Oxford**. From historical buildings to beautiful parks, Thame has a rich heritage and continues to thrive today with regular markets throughout the year.

Cross the rolling Chiltern Hills, perfect for a picnic or a meandering stroll. Enjoy a trip on the **Chinnor and Princes Risborough Steam Railway**, and travel the scenic route in style along the hills. Stop at **Didcot Railway Centre** to see a unique collection of **Great Western Railway** steam engines.

NATURE LOVERS

FAMILIES

HISTORY

Use the River Rapids itinerary to journey through South Oxfordshire Read More | p.68 ►

Visit **Henley-on-Thames (♀ E6 County)**, home to the famous **Henley Royal Regatta** and one of the most beautiful towns in **Oxfordshire**. Its riverside location, surrounded by a landscape of wooded hills and green fields, lends itself to relaxation.

Wallingford (♀ D5 County) has been important historically due to its excellent ford, and today the same crossing place has one of the finest bridges over the River Thames. Learn more about Wallingford's former resident **Dame Agatha Christie** in a circular walk taking in places linked to the author.

1 ► *Wallingford*
2 ► *Steam Railway*
  credit:
  Peter Harris
3 ► *Henley*
  credit:
  James Finlay
4 ► *Chiltern Hills*

50 YEARS
Cotswold Wildlife Park & Gardens
1970 - 2020

Closer to Wildlife

SAVE! WITH E-TICKETS

Burford, Oxfordshire.
www.cotswoldwildlifepark.co.uk

VALE OF WHITE HORSE
Ancient Beauty

1 ►

The **Vale of White Horse** stretches from the edge of **Oxford** to the threshold of the **Cotswolds**. Its enchanting landscape is marked by a mysterious pagan past - the very name comes from the oldest chalk figure in **Britain**, dating back over 3000 years.

The landscape's beauty has inspired poets, painters and musicians. It offers many walking and cycling trails. Mile upon mile of the **Thames Path** leads you to wonderful waterside pubs, hidden villages and glorious countryside. **Waylands Smithy** is one of the most impressive prehistoric tombs in Britain.

Abingdon-on-Thames (♀ **D5 County**) is the largest town in the Vale and can be reached by foot from the Thames Path or by boat from the **River Thames**. With a wealth of history to be discovered, Abingdon makes a great base from which to explore the Vale.

Wantage (♀ **C5 County**) is an ancient market town and birthplace of **King Alfred the Great**. Visit the award-winning **Downland Museum** which tells the story of the **White Horse**. **Grove**, on the outskirts of Wantage, has grown from a settlement recorded in the **Doomsday Book**. Enjoy a stroll along **Letcombe Brook** to discover a host of wildlife.

Faringdon (♀ **B5 County**) has been welcoming visitors for many centuries. Take a break in one of the quirky coffee shops, or climb to the top of the hill above Faringdon to see the gothic **Folly tower** and views across four counties.

Great for

HISTORY

FAMILIES

HIDDEN GEMS

Journey through the Vale of White Horse using the Ridgeway Trail itinerary
Read More | p.70 ►

2 ►

1 ► *The White Horse*
2 ► *Wantage*

WEST OXFORDSHIRE
Gateway to the Cotswolds

West Oxfordshire is characterised by the rolling hills of the **Cotswolds**, offering excitement for any visitor.

Burford (**♀ B4 County**) is an ancient town nestled in the countryside. Stroll down the picturesque **High Street**, lined with idyllic stone cottages, boutiques, pubs and restaurants. Explore Burford's alleyways and lanes where you can immerse yourself in medieval history and charm.

For a walk on the wild side, **Cotswold Wildlife Park & Gardens** (**♀ B4 County**) is within close reach of Burford, and offers fantastic fun. The Wildlife Park is home to over 300 animal species, stunning gardens, a giraffe walk-way, a large adventure playground and many events throughout the year.

Experience timeless Cotswolds life at **Cogges Manor Farm** (**♀ C4 County**) and stroll around the picnic orchard and walled garden of the historic farmstead. Pick up vegetables from the farm's reception and have fun feeding the friendly farm animals! Visitors can also enjoy Victorian cooking demonstrations, craft sessions and croquet on the lawn.

Woodstock (**♀ C3 County**) is a picturesque Georgian town located on the edge of the **Oxfordshire Cotswolds**, containing many attractive honey stone buildings. It's a great base from which to explore the county, within reach of **Oxford** and the Cotswold countryside. The town borders the estate of magnificent **Blenheim Palace** (**♀ C3 County**), and in the centre of Woodstock are the **Oxfordshire Museum** and **Soldiers of Oxfordshire Museum**. Stop by the **Macdonald Bear Hotel**, a 13th century coaching inn, for a spot of lunch or afternoon tea, just a short walk from Blenheim Palace.

Great for

FAMILIES

HIDDEN GEMS

NATURE LOVERS

Use our Woodstock to Burford itinerary to journey through West Oxfordshire Read More | p.74 ➤

1 ➤ *Burford*
2 ➤ *Cogges Manor Farm*
3 ➤ *Blenheim Palace*

OXFORDSHIRE'S
Screen and Literary Links

Oxfordshire has been the location for countless films and TV series, and has also been the inspiration for some of the world's best-loved novels and characters.

Great for

CULTURE

HIDDEN GEMS

HISTORY

Feel like you're in Downton Abbey with a decadent afternoon tea
Read More | p.36 ►

HARRY POTTER

Much of the *Harry Potter* series was filmed in Oxford. Wander through the cobbled streets of **Oxford** and visit the magical places that were brought to life. At **Christ Church College** (**9 D4 City**), you'll find the Tudor dining hall which provided inspiration for Hogwarts' **Great Hall**. See if you can spot the area where Harry spent time recovering in the **Hogwarts Infirmary** when you visit the **Divinity School**, or the location where Draco **Malfoy** was turned into a ferret by **Mad-Eye Moody** under the giant oak tree in **New College**.

DOWNTON ABBEY

The **Oxfordshire Cotswolds** and its picturesque villages frequently appeared in the popular TV drama. **Bampton** plays the part of the Yorkshire village of **Downton** in every series, and **Cogges Manor Farm** (**9 C4 County**) may also be better known as **Yew Tree Farm**.

HIS DARK MATERIALS

Author **Philip Pullman** has been inspired by Oxford, having studied at **Exeter College** during the 1960s, and still lives in the city today. Exeter College may be better known to readers as **Jordan College**. **Godstow Abbey**, the **Trout Inn** and the **Botanic Gardens** also feature in Pullman's literary works. Step into the world of the BBC/HBO adaptation by visiting **Oxford Botanic Garden**, The **Bridge of Sighs** (**♥ E3 City**) and **New College**, which moonlights in the TV adaptation as Jordan College.

AGATHA CHRISTIE

Dame Agatha Christie is loved worldwide for her compelling crime novels and famous sleuths; including **Hercule Poirot** and **Miss Marple**. **Wallingford** (**♥ D5 County**) was the home of Christie, and the inspiration for much of her work. Visit **Wallingford Museum**'s exhibition '*At Home with the Queen of Crime*' to learn fascinating details about the life and work of one of the most famous novelists of all time.

ALICE IN WONDERLAND

Charles Dodgson, better known as **Lewis Carroll**, wrote his famous tales of *Alice in Wonderland* in Oxford, the city where Carroll lived and studied for nearly fifty years. The dining hall of **Christ Church College** houses treasures associated with the whimsical tales; see if you can spot the stained-glass window where **Alice**, the **Cheshire Cat** and other characters feature, and the wooden chair with the Cheshire Cat's wide smile carved into it. When leaving Christ Church onto **St Aldates**, you will find **Alice's Shop**, where the real Alice bought sweets as a young girl. A landmark for Alice enthusiasts, Alice's Shop featured as **The Old Sheep Shop** in *Alice Through the Looking-Glass* and was even illustrated by **Tenniel** in the first edition of the book.

Some Oxfordshire traditions are as quirky as Alice in Wonderland! Read More | p.40 ➤

MIDSOMER MURDERS

Follow in the footsteps of **Inspector Barnaby of Causton CID** and the characters of the hugely popular detective series. Discover the various filming locations - particularly **Wallingford**, which served as the drama's fictional town of **Causton**. **Thame** (**♥ E4 County**), at the foot of the **Chiltern Hills**, also frequently features.

1 ➤ *Christ Church Hall*
credit: Ralph Williamson
2 ➤ *Bampton Church*
3 ➤ *Exeter College*
4 ➤ *Alice's Shop*

INSPECTOR MORSE, LEWIS AND ENDEAVOUR

The city of Oxford is the setting for the books and TV series of *Inspector Morse* and *Lewis*, and most recently *Endeavour*. Enjoy a drink at the **Morse Bar** in the **Randolph Hotel** (**♀ C2 City**) or the **White Horse Pub** where the detectives spent time deliberating over cases. Amble along the **River Thames** where many bodies were hidden, sit on the steps of the **Ashmolean Museum** (**♀ C2 City**), the location of many scenes, or visit **Exeter College** where Morse had his fatal heart attack.

Spot many of these sites during a 2-day visit to Oxford
Read More | p.62 ➤

THE CHRONICLES OF NARNIA

C.S. Lewis studied at **University College** and was later appointed English Fellow and Tutor at **Magdalen College**. It was here that he wrote the beloved children's series, the *Chronicles of Narnia*. Visit **St Mary's Passage** and see if you can spot the carved fawn in one of the door frames, the inspiration for **Mr Tumnus**. Keep an eye out around the city for lampposts made by **Lucy & Co**!

LORD OF THE RINGS

Walk in the footsteps of legendary *Lord of the Rings* author **J.R.R. Tolkien** in Oxford. Relax with a drink in **Keepers Kitchen and Bar**, as Tolkien did with friend and fellow member of the **Inklings** writing group C.S. Lewis. Wander among the greenery of **Oxford Botanic Garden**, where Tolkien used to spend time, or visit **Exeter College**, where Tolkien studied for his undergraduate degree. Immerse yourself in culture at the **History of Science Museum** - Tolkien worked on words near the beginning of the letter W for the First Edition of the **Oxford English Dictionary** in the same building - or at the **Ashmolean Museum** (**♀ C2 City**), which houses a collection of gold rings thought to be the inspiration for **The One Ring**.

1 ➤ *Randolph Morse Bar* credit: Adrian Wroth

2 ➤ *St Mary's Passage*

3 ➤ *Magdalen College*

ADVICE
From the Locals

There is so much to see and do in Oxfordshire, it's tricky knowing where to start! We asked local Oxfordshire people to pick out their favourite places to go, from essential first-time-visit spots to hidden gems.

Great for

HIDDEN GEMS

ADVENTURERS

CULTURE

VEGAN SPOTS IN THE CITY

*At first glance, it might seem like **Oxford** doesn't have many options for vegetarians and vegans. On closer inspection, though, you'll find that it's easy to eat plant-based in the city! I'd recommend heading to **Jericho**, where pubs like **The Fir Tree** and **The Gardener's Arms** have some really tasty vegan dishes, or **Cowley**, where you'll find Oxford's first 100% vegan restaurant, **Happy Friday Kitchen**".*
- **RHYS FROM OXFORD**

BROWSE A BOOKSHOP

*I could spend an eternity at **Blackwell's Bookshop** on **Broad Street**. Their collection of books is huge, you could while away an entire afternoon browsing the miles of shelves in the shop".*
- **ROBERT FROM SUMMERTOWN**

GET YOUR BEARINGS

*When I moved to Oxford a few years ago I went on an **Oxford Official Walking Tour** which gave me a very good introduction to the history of the city and university. Each time my friends visit Oxford and we have a stroll through the city they say there is something magical about it that makes you want to come back!"*
- **HAYLEY FROM KIDLINGTON**

EXPLORE BANBURY

> Banbury (📍 **C2 County**) is a little market town in the north of Oxfordshire. It's home to the 16th century **Ye Olde Reindeer Inn**, used by **Oliver Cromwell** as a base during the **Civil War**, and the 18th century **Tooley's Boatyard**, where you can take a guided tour of the narrow boat workshop beside the canal. Banbury is ideal as a base to travel to **Warwickshire** and **Stratford-Upon-Avon**, and nearby **Broughton Castle** (📍 **C2 County**), so I would recommend it to anyone visiting Oxfordshire!"
> - **ANTONIO FROM BANBURY**

Advice From the Locals

No visit to Oxfordshire is complete without ticking the top 10 visitor attractions off your list
Read More | p.6 ►

ALL ABOUT THE VIEWS

> I never get bored of the view over Oxford's skyline - the dreaming spires always spark my imagination. The best places to take in the view are from **Westgate** shopping centre's (📍 **C4 City**) roof terrace, the rooftop restaurant at the **Ashmolean,** or **The Varsity Club** bar in the **Covered Market** (📍 **D3 City**)."
> - **ANNIE FROM WITNEY**

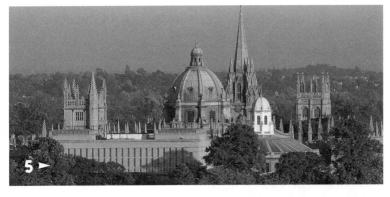

Why not spend an evening experiencing Oxford's nightlife?
Read More | p.58 ►

HIDDEN GEM BY THE THAMES

> I am a big fan of the **Abingdon Museum** (📍 **D5 County**) in the famous county hall built in 1682. You can look down from the museum galleries and watch the crowds of people in the market square below. There's always something going on in **Abingdon's Market Square** too!"
> - **SAM FROM ABINGDON**

AFROON TEA
in Oxfordshire

There's nothing more refined and delectable than enjoying a classic afternoon tea surrounded by the lush Oxfordshire countryside or the beautiful City of Dreaming Spires. Fortunately, there are numerous venues to discover - each with something unique to enjoy! We've highlighted a few places guaranteed to tickle your tastebuds.

Great for

FOOD & DRINKS

CULTURE

HIDDEN GEMS

THE OLD PARSONAGE

A renowned **Oxford** institution originating from the 17th century, the **Old Parsonage** provides a truly traditional setting in which to revel in their various afternoon teas - including a champagne option! The stylish dining room delivers a deliciously intimate feel with its stunning original portraits, roaring log fire and comfortable seating area. (📍 **C2 City**)

BLENHEIM PALACE

Make your afternoon tea experience even more enjoyable and truly unforgettable with a relaxing visit to one of **Blenheim Palace's** onsite dining establishments. The decadent **Orangery Restaurant** offers guests a **Traditional**

Afternoon Tea with stunning close-up views of the **Duke of Marlborough's** private Italian gardens, whilst **The Oxfordshire Pantry** provides fresh, homemade cakes, tea and coffee that can be taken away with you to enjoy on the Palace lawns. (📍 **C3 County**)

VINTAGE DAYS OUT

To enjoy your tea in privacy, take to the river with **Vintage Days Out** and their fleet of superbly-restored vintage boats. Watch the afternoon drift by as you relax and take in the sights, including the local wildlife that inhabit the water's edge. You'll have your own professional chef on board preparing fresh picnic lunches, cream tea and luxury buffets -

a bespoke day out perfect for celebrations and special events.

THE RANDOLPH HOTEL

The epitome of English style and charm, the **Drawing Room and Lounge** at the **Randolph Hotel** is the perfect setting for their famous afternoon teas. They are proud to serve afternoon tea at its very best, with a delicious selection of savoury finger sandwiches, fluffy scones with jam and clotted cream, an array of delicate cakes and more. Their afternoon tea is perfect for a special occasion or even after a busy day sightseeing or shopping. (**C2 City**)

Combine an afternoon tea with a fun event for an unforgettable day in Oxfordshire
Read More | p.46 ►

MALMAISON

Get together for an indulgent afternoon at **Malmaison**, a boutique hotel in a converted prison located in **Oxford Castle Quarter**. Malmaison serve reimagined afternoon tea classics, such as a Battenberg slice and Coronation chicken wrap; choose a classic cream tea or the full afternoon tea, then add a cocktail or Champagne and relax for the rest of the afternoon. It would be a crime not to. (**C4 City**)

BLETCHLEY PARK

Head out to **Bletchley Park** for afternoon tea in their iconic mansion house. Set in the elegant Victorian dining room where the World War II codebreakers dined,

enjoy finely cut sandwiches and freshly-baked scones served on vintage china, followed by a delectable selection of delicate pastries and other homemade delights. (**F2 County**)

A CITY BUILT ON THE WATER
Exploring Oxford's rivers and canals

Great for

NATURE LOVERS

FAMILIES

ADVENTURERS

No visit to Oxford is complete without exploring the city's waterways - the mighty River Thames which flows through to London, the River Cherwell and the historic Oxford Canal, now over 200 years old.

The waterways offer an opportunity to explore the hidden side of the city, take part in exciting activities and to see the city from a different perspective.

Visit our website for more information, local contacts, maps and guides. exox.org/oxfords-waterways

EXPLORE THE OXFORD CANAL

A short walk from the city centre takes you to the start of the **Oxford Canal**. Dug by hand over 200 years ago, it runs for 77 miles. It was an important trade route, with the unique narrow boats originally pulled by horses carrying goods to London and the rest of the country.

Now it is an oasis of peace and quiet. Take a walk along the towpath you will see wildlife, passing boats and can learn about the canal's history as you follow the **Oxford Canal Heritage Trail**.

You can even hire a narrowboat for a day trip or longer and really explore with **College Cruisers**.

EXPLORE THE RIVER THAMES

Just a short walk from the city is the famous **Head of the River** public house and **Folly Bridge** over the **Thames**, which marks the finish line for university rowing races. Walk along the towpath and you will often see the Oxford University rowing crews practicing and may be lucky enough to watch a race.

Visiting **Christ Church Meadow** is a must-do, with its circular path taking you alongside both the Thames and the **River Cherwell**.

Nothing can beat a walk around **Port Meadow**, an ancient area of grazing with incredible open views across the Thames, wildlife and cosy local pubs.

The **Thames Path National Trail** also comes through Oxford on its 183-mile route from the source of the Thames all the way to London. Oxford is an excellent base to explore it in sections.

THINGS TO DO - MESSING ABOUT ON THE RIVER

Enjoy a different view of Oxford by getting onto the water.

You must try punting - the unique flat-bottomed boats you push along with a pole (take champagne and strawberries for a traditional picnic afloat!). There are several places you can hire one on both the River Thames and River Cherwell.

If you have time to explore further, take a boat trip. **Salter's Steamers** offer regular passenger ferries along the Thames, stopping at several points and continuing on to **Abingdon**, the UK's oldest town. You can take the boat back, or jump off along the way and enjoy a walk back to the city along the Thames Path, or you can even take your bicycles. Salter's also rent out small motor-boats you can sail yourself.

The Folly River Cafe and Restaurant offers special cruises with drinks and dining, exploring the Thames right up to Port Meadow.

PLACES TO EAT AND DRINK

There are many fantastic places alongside Oxford's waterways for a drink, a quick lunch or a full three-course and more dinner.

Visit our website for a full list of waterside cafés, pubs and restaurants.

OXFORD'S WATERWAYS LOOP WALK

Following the historic canal from the centre, a short 2-mile walking route takes you along the canal and then across to Port Meadow, with its open skies and views, then back to the city alongside the River Thames.

For a longer and more complete experience, the 7-mile route continues to the village of **Wolvercote**, with its local shop and cosy pubs. Back along the Thames Path National Trail, with views right across Port Meadow, and into the city again. Go out for a pub lunch and enjoy a walk back.

Visit the website for a map and further information:
exox.org/oxfords-waterways

Love being on the water? Continue your journey north through Oxfordshire on the Oxford Canal

Read More | p.66 ➤

Or journey south along the River Thames

Read More | p.68 ➤

1 ➤ *Magdalen College Rowing Boat*
credit: Sarah Rhodes

2 ➤ *Oxford Canal*
credit: Georgia Melodie Hole

3 ➤ *Head of the River*

4 ➤ *River Thames at Osney*
credit: Sarah Rhodes

ONLY IN OXFORDSHIRE
Quirky Traditions

Great for

HIDDEN GEMS

ADVENTURERS

CULTURE

Want to catch the students in their gowns and finery? Read our tips on when best to visit the University of Oxford
Read More | p.52 ►

Oxfordshire is home to an array of quirky traditions that make the county unique.

MERTON COLLEGE TIME CEREMONY

Once a year, on the night the clocks go back, students of **Merton College** partake in the tradition of the **Merton College Time Ceremony**. Created by undergraduates in 1971, the ceremony involves students dressing in full academic dress whilst walking backwards around the **Fellows' Quad** with a glass of port in their hand, from 02:00BST for an hour until 02:00GMT, to allegedly maintain the space-time continuum.

POOH STICKS

Once a year Oxfordshire hosts the **World Pooh Sticks Championships** in **Witney**. Taking inspiration from the beloved children's book, **Winnie the Pooh**, anybody can take part to become the Pooh Sticks world champion. You just need to pick your stick and drop it upstream on one side of a bridge and whoever's stick appears on the other side of the bridge is the winner!

MAY MORNING

One of **Oxford's** well-loved traditions, held every year on the 1st of May, sees citywide celebrations for the coming of Spring, bringing the community together for what is known as **May Morning**. Morris Men dance across the city, and the choristers of **Magdalen College** choir sing the day in from the **Great Tower** at 6am with **Hymnus

Eucharisticus, attracting flocks of people to **Magdalen Bridge** before celebrations continue throughout the morning.

BUN THROWING

Bun Throwing in Abingdon is a famous tradition in Oxfordshire dating back 400 years. Local dignitaries throw currant buns from the Abingdon County Hall Museum on days of celebration; attracting huge crowds all hoping to catch a bun!

THE CORPUS CHRISTI TORTOISE FAIR

Corpus Christi's Tortoise Fair is one of the lovelier eccentricities at Oxford and has at its heart the **Tortoise Race,** in which tortoises from various colleges race to get to the edge of a ring of lettuce. It's thought to have been started in the 1920s. Corpus's own tortoises are named Oldham and Foxe - whose care is presided over by a **"Custos Testudinum"** or **"Tortoise Keeper"**, elected at the start of each year.

1 ► *May Day*
2 ► *Bun Throwing*

JUNKYARD GOLF CLUB

CRAZY GOLF

JUST GOT EPIC

GET EXCITED ON 3 MASHED UP CRAZY GOLF COURSES!

BOOK TO PUTT:

WWW.JUNKYARDGOLFCLUB.CO.UK

FIND US INSIDE WESTGATE

Due to technical difficulties your favourite radio stations are **still** broadcasting across Oxfordshire

Oxfordshire

THE PLACE TO CELEBRATE

With over 100 venues to choose from, including iconic palaces, stately homes, rural barns, barges and fabulous hotels, Oxfordshire is THE place to marry.

For further information, visit
www.oxfordshire.gov.uk/marriages
or call
0345 241 2489

VICTORS
RESTAURANT & BAR

Visit Victors

Overlooking the famous spires of Oxford, beautiful, vibrant, upscale yet informal, Victors is the perfect neighbourhood restaurant. Offering a modern American menu of small and larger plates - perfect to share in a casually elegant setting, with service to match.

Victors is the perfect spot to while away a few hours over coffee, lunch, cocktails and dinner or a spot of brunch at the weekend.

Book Now

@victors_restaurants | www.victors.co.uk

YOUR OXFORDSHIRE STORY

1 ►

Find our recommended itineraries
Read More | p.62 onwards ►

Whether you're visiting **Oxfordshire** from near or far, the county has so much to offer that we're sure you'll want to make the most of it. So, we've crafted some inspiring itineraries to help you plan your visit - whether you want an action-packed minibreak in **Oxford** or a peaceful week exploring the beautiful countryside of the county.

Maybe you'd like to time your visit to include one of the UK's top music festivals, or perhaps seeing **University of Oxford** students graduating in their academic robes is on your bucket list. We've highlighted the key dates you need to know about, so that you don't miss the best events of the year.

Oxfordshire is only an hour away from **London** via train and has great links to many top attractions in the UK - making the county a fantastic base for your trip to **England**. Take a day trip to **Stonehenge**, **Bath** or **Stratford-Upon-Avon**, before putting on your dancing shoes to enjoy Oxford's vibrant nightlife.

These are just ideas - Oxfordshire is yours to make your own. If you need help, let our friendly **Visitor Information Centre** team help you plan your visit by calling **+44(0)1865 686430** or email **info@experienceoxfordshire.org**.

Venture off the beaten track with our local tips
Read More | p.34 ►

Whatever you're up to in Oxfordshire, use #ExperienceOx on social media to share your experiences with us. We'd love to hear from you!

Not sure when to visit? Check our What's On pages for some inspiration
Read More | p.46 ►

#ExperienceOx

We are very sociable!

Follow us on Facebook, Instagram and Twitter

 @ExperienceOx

 @experienceoxfordshire

 @experienceoxfordshire

1 ► *Blenheim Palace*

WHAT'S ON
2020

Come rain or shine, and no matter the time of year, we guarantee there's always an exciting adventure to be had throughout Oxfordshire.

For full details of these and even more events, visit **exox.org/whats-on**

Type of event

OUTDOORS

FAMILY FRIENDLY

ARTS

HISTORIC

FOOD & DRINK

MUSIC & SHOWS

46

Spring

Enjoy impressive displays of Spring flowering bulbs at Batsford Aboretum, Waterperry Gardens or Oxford's parks - from swathes of bluebells, snowdrops and daffodils to the beautiful blossom of magnolias and flowering cherries. Go punting on the River Cherwell or cycling in the Cotswold countryside, or immerse yourself in culture at a literary festival, museum exhibition or concert.

For full details of these and even more events, visit exox.org/whats-on

---

15ᵗʰ Feb - 13ᵗʰ Apr
Let's Misbehave - The 1920's at Blenheim Palace
A fascinating insight into the heady world of the upper classes in a time of great social, artistic and political change.
blenheimpalace.com/whats-on

21ˢᵗ Feb, 26ᵗʰ-29ᵗʰ Feb
Torpids
Cheer on the Oxford colleges at the annual Torpids rowing and bumping races.
ourcs.co.uk

27ᵗʰ Feb - 7ᵗʰ Jun
Young Rembrandt Exhibition at the Ashmolean Museum
This major exhibition will be the first in the UK to explore the early years of the career of the most famous of all Dutch artists, Rembrandt van Rijn.
ashmolean.org/youngrembrandt

27ᵗʰ Mar - 5ᵗʰ Apr
Oxford Literary Festival
Over 350 writers flock to the famous university city to discuss affairs literary, political, historical, environmental and culinary.
oxfordliteraryfestival.org

1ˢᵗ May
May Morning
At 6am Oxford will be woken with the choristers of Magdalen College choir singing Hymnus Eucharisticus from the Great Tower. Celebrations of the coming of Spring will flow throughout Oxford, with Morris Men dancing and activities spread across the city.
Oxford.gov.uk

May Day

2ⁿᵈ - 3ʳᵈ May
Jousting Tournament
A weekend packed with action and entertainment, with knights on horseback charging in traditional tilt and battling on foot with the mighty mace and quarterstaff!
blenheimpalace.com/whats-on

2nd - 25th May

Oxfordshire Artweeks

Meet hundreds of artists, craftspeople and designer-makers in a range of venues across Oxfordshire during this unique festival that celebrates art in Oxfordshire.
artweeks.org

 3rd May

Town & Gown Run

Whether you're a serious athlete or a beginner, run a 10k or 3k scenic route through Oxford city centre with around 5,000 other runners.
townandgown10k.com/oxford

 25th May

Cogges Family Festival

A celebration of family fun at Cogges. Story corner, puppet show, cookery sessions, circus skills, arts and crafts, games and forest school.
cogges.org.uk

 28th May - 18th Jul

Garsington Opera Festival

Celebrate summer at the Garsington Opera Festival with four fantastic productions to choose from.
garsingtonopera.org

 30th May

Oxford Pride Parade

Oxford Pride's annual parade, starting at midday from Radcliffe Square and travelling through the city to the Castle Quarter.
oxford-pride.org.uk

Summer

If you're not too busy enjoying picnics and barbecues, there are many activities, events and tours happening throughout the county this summer. Oxford welcomes many festivals and street carnivals, notably Alice's Day and Cowley Road Carnival. Returning for its eighth year in June, the Blenheim Palace Flower Show celebrates the very best of gardening, home and lifestyle. Plus, discover plenty of festivals to keep you dancing long after the summer sun has set.

For full details of these and even more events, visit exox.org/whats-on

 6th - 14th Jun

Oxford Green Week

A summer festival which uses culture, creativity and community to a celebrate all things good and green in Oxford and inspire people to take action against climate change.
oxfordgreenweek.org

 6th - 14th Jun

Oxford Bike Week

Get on your bike for a range of rides and events during Oxford Bike Week. Open for all to join.
oxfordbikeweek.co.uk

 24th - 28th Jun

Offbeat Festival

Offbeat is a festival of new comedy, theatre, family shows, dance, spoken word and music, taking place at the Old Fire Station and Oxford Playhouse.
offbeatoxford.co.uk

 25th - 28th Jun

Handmade in Oxford

Handmade in Oxford offers the opportunity to discover the crafts of local artists in Waterperry Gardens.
waterperrygardens.co.uk

26th - 28th Jun

Blenheim Palace Flower Show

Get inspiration for your home and garden from this wonderful three-day flower show.
blenheimflowershow.co.uk

1st - 5th Jul

Henley Royal Regatta

Spend a summer's day down by the Thames at the sophisticated and exciting Henley Royal Regatta.
hrr.co.uk

4th Jul

Alice's Day

Every year, Oxford comes together to commemorate Lewis Carroll's enchanting tales of Alice in Wonderland with a variety of magically whimsical activities throughout the day.
storymuseum.org.uk

Alice's Day

47

5th Jul

Cowley Road Carnival

Join the buzzing crowds for another year of the Cowley Road Carnival, celebrating community and culture in Oxford.
cowleyroadcarnival.co.uk

 31st Jul - 2nd Aug

Truck Festival

Watch an array of the best emerging local and national music talent at Truck Festival 2020.
truckfestival.com

 28th - 30th Aug

The Big Feastival

Fantastically family-friendly food and music festival near Chipping Norton.
thebigfeastival.com

 10th - 12th Jul

Cornbury Music Festival

A country fair with a rock 'n' roll twist, Cornbury Music Festival is a family event not to be missed.
cornburyfestival.com

 13th - 15th Aug

Fairport's Cropredy Convention

Cropredy's annual folk and rock festival, organised by the band Fairport Convention.
fairportconvention.com

 30th - 31st Aug

Uffington White Horse Show

Get your adrenaline pumping with attractions including aeroplanes, helicopters, BMX and heavy horse displays.
whitehorseshow.co.uk

 30th Jul - 2nd Aug

Wilderness Festival

Wilderness Festival is the multi-award-winning 4-day festival of live music, wild swimming, spectacle, late night revelry and dining experiences.
wildernessfestival.com

Oxford Skyline

Autumn

Savour the last sunny days before the cool, crisp air takes over. Look out for seasonal apple or pumpkin days at Cogges Manor Farm or Waterperry Gardens, where you can sample the season's bounty. Or, revel in the vivid colours and enjoy a crisp walk in the countryside. Enjoy a walk across the ancient chalk downs of Oxfordshire and absorb the history found along the ancient Ridgeway.

For full details of these and even more events, visit exox.org/whats-on

 7th - 8th Sep

St Giles Fair

The annual St Giles fair in central Oxford dates back to 1625. The fair is one of the greatest funfairs in the country, and features dozens of exciting rides, food stalls and games.
oxford.gov.uk/info/20013/about_oxford/557/st_giles_fair

 11th - 12th Sep

Oxford Canal Festival

Wander down to the water for a wonderful celebration of the Oxford Canal and its colourful history, including a range of family-friendly activities and entertainment.
oxfordcanalheritage.org/oxford-canal-festival-2020

 12th - 13th Sep

Oxford Open Doors

Discover Oxford's history and fall in love with the city all over again during this very special weekend event.
oxfordpreservation.org.uk/content/oxford-open-doors

26th - 27th Sep
Thame Food Festival
Tuck into delicious artisan food and street food. Expect demonstrations from top chefs, food stalls and artisan drinks offerings.
thamefoodfestival.co.uk

16th - 26th Oct
IF Oxford Science and Ideas Festival
Everyone can learn something new at the Oxford Science and Ideas festival, with events covering all levels of interest.
if-oxford.com

28th Sep - 6th Oct
Henley Literary Festival
As one of the biggest book festivals in the UK, Henley Literary Festival is an unmissable event for anyone with a passion for literature.
henleyliteraryfestival.co.uk

22nd - 25th Oct
Blenheim Palace Festival of Literature, Film and Music
Join in with a full programme of exciting events, bringing together great minds in the fields of literature and culture.
blenheimpalaceliteraryfestival.com

Blenheim Palace

Winter

Winter is a memorable and magical time to be in Oxfordshire. Wake up to frosty mornings and slowly make your way to a traditional pub with a roaring log fire by mid-afternoon. Whether you're in the city or countryside, there are plenty of traditional inns and world-class restaurants to warm up in.

For full details of these and even more events, visit exox.org/whats-on

20th - 22nd Nov
Oxford Christmas Lights Festival
With the countdown nearly on, celebrate everything Christmas in Oxford at this year's Christmas Lights Festival.
oxlightfest.com

3rd - 20th Dec
Oxford Christmas Market
The city of dreaming spires will again be filled with festive joy as the Oxford Christmas Market returns to the heart of the city on beautiful and historic Broad Street.
oxfordchristmasmarket.co.uk

Randolph Hotel

49

THE RANDOLPH HOTEL

STAY IN THE HEART OF OXFORD

—

Oxford's leading hotel, the historic Randolph offers luxe accommodations and world-class dining. With an unrivaled dedication to seasonality and sourcing, our all-day restaurant champions fresh fish and seafood alongside British game and steaks. It's the perfect setting for comfort and indulgence in the heart of Oxford. While you're with us, explore Oxford University and take in the town's rich offerings.

A UNIVERSITY OF OXFORD YEAR

Great for

CULTURE

HISTORY

HIDDEN GEMS

With ornate buildings, pristine quads and grand dining halls, stepping into a University of Oxford college is like stepping into another world. The students of the University come and go from their colleges every day, but these annual University occasions give you a sneak peek into student life.

In the Autumn, around mid-October, Oxford students make their way to **The Sheldonian Theatre** (📍 **D3 City**) in their academic robes, or "Sub Fusc", for 'Matriculation'; the official ceremony welcoming new students to the University, which is performed solely in Latin.

As the summer months draw near, you'll see the students nervously walking toward the **Examination Schools**, again in their Sub Fusc robes, for their exams in June.

Also in June, glimpse the **University of Oxford's** most prestigious annual ceremony, *Encaenia*, when the University awards honorary degrees to distinguished men and women.

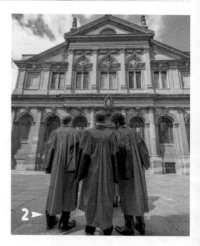

Some participants, including the Chancellor and Vice-Chancellor, take part in a procession through Radcliffe Square and the **Divinity School** to the **Sheldonian Theatre**, where the ceremony takes place.

To celebrate the end of the University year, colleges throw extravagant balls for their students. In the summer evening breeze, see students' ball gowns and tails fluttering as they arrive at their college balls.

In mid-Summer and towards early Autumn, catch the students throwing their mortarboards in the air as they celebrate their graduation!

1 ➤ *Brasenose Lane*
credit: Sarah Rhodes

2&3 ➤ *Sheldonian*

WESTGATE

FUN, FOOD AND FASHION

Home to over 100 stores featuring the best of the British Highstreet and prestigious global brands. **Just a 5 minute walk from the city.**

OXFORD

OXFORDSHIRE
County Map

━━━━━━━━━ **MAIN ROADS**

┼┼┼┼┼┼┼┼┼┼┼┼ **TRAIN LINES**

└ 2mi ┆ 5km ┘ **SCALE**

· · · · · · · · · · **DISTANCE FROM OXFORD**

▢ **GRID SQUARE = 9.3mi/15km**

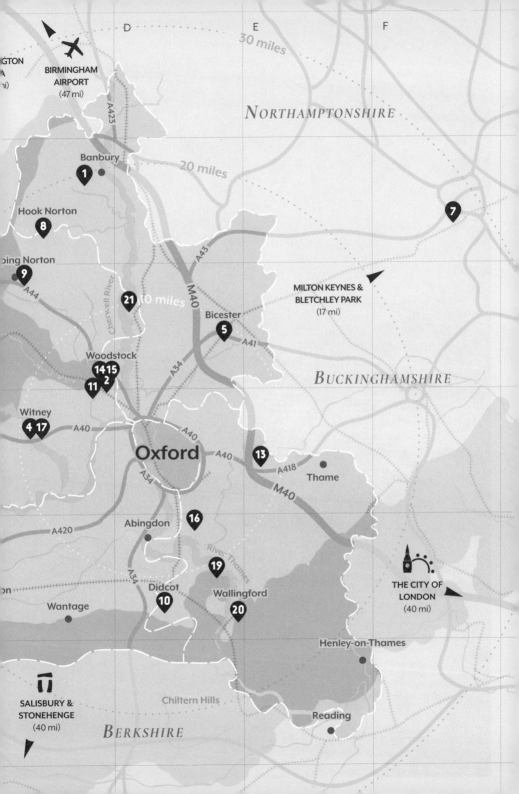

FIVE GO O

GREAT WEST

ADVENTU

STAYING OVER IN OXFORD
Nightlife in the city

From traditional pubs to buzzing bars, live performances to late night clubs and everything in between, there are plenty of things to see and do in this vibrant city once the sun goes down.

Great for

ADVENTURERS

FOOD & DRINK

CULTURE

Find restaurants, bars and hotels in our listings pages
Read More | p.87 ►

OXFORD CASTLE QUARTER

Next door to ancient **Oxford Castle**, **Oxford Castle Quarter** (**♥ C4 City**) is home to a selection of restaurants and bars.

Oxford's prison used to be on this site but is now the boutique **Malmaison** hotel, which is a great place to stay the night in a converted prison cell.

WESTGATE

Westgate shopping centre's (**♥ C4 City**) atmospheric roof terrace is a perfect backdrop for an eclectic mix of fine and contemporary casual restaurants and bars, including **Pho**, **Victors**, **The Alchemist** and **Cinnamon Kitchen**. With unique views of Oxford's dreaming spires, Westgate's roof terrace is the ultimate destination in the city. Or, try your luck at **Junkyard Golf Club**, Oxford's indoor golf course and bar. Their unique and bizarre golf courses will always leave you laughing!

EAST OXFORD

Towards the east of Oxford, **Cowley Road** and **St Clements** are a vibrant hub for nightlife. With buzzing bars, restaurants offering a variety of contemporary cuisines, and fantastic live music destinations, from larger clubs to basement gig spots, **East Oxford** is a treasure trove for things to do in the evening.

Staying Over in Oxford

Stay in Oxford overnight and take a day trip to a top visitor attraction during your stay Read More | p.78 ►

THEATRE

Immerse yourself in Oxford's thriving arts and culture scene with a touch of drama or comedy; Oxford's larger theatres the **Oxford Playhouse** and **New Theatre** (📍 **C3 City**) feature both student and professional productions. For independent performances, the **Old Fire Station** and **North Wall Arts Centre** put on incredible productions and events.

PUBS AND BARS

Mingle with intellectuals in Oxford's bars and pubs. From cocktail bars renowned for expertly-mixed aperitifs, sophisticated piano bars and wine cafes, to rooftop venues offering sweeping views of Oxford's skyline, Oxford has a wide selection of bars. For something more low-key, relax in some of the oldest pubs in Britain. We recommend **The Turf Tavern**, **The Eagle & Child** and **The Bear** in the city centre, or relax on the bank of the **River Thames** at **The Head of the River**.

Find upcoming events at **exox.org/whats-on** or by searching **#experienceox** on social media

1 ► *Malmaison*
2&3 ► *Westgate*
4&5 ► *Oxford Playhouse*
6 ► *Turf Tavern*
7 ► *Head of the River*

CHORAL EVENSONG

If you wander around Oxford in the evening, as you pass the **University of Oxford** college chapels you'll hear the faint music of the college choirs singing. Immerse yourself in the experience of **Choral Evensong**, which happens every evening during University term-time and starts between 5:15pm and 6:45pm depending on which college you visit.

CLASSICAL MUSIC CONCERTS

Oxford's streets are often lined with signs and posters advertising upcoming classical music concerts - Oxford's stunning and historic venues play host to a busy calendar of concerts and recitals. See world-renowned musicians and artists play in intimate venues such as the **Holywell Music Room**, said to be the oldest purpose-built music room in Europe.

1 ▶

JAZZ

Dance the night away at lively jazz concerts in unique venues such as **The Mad Hatter**, an eccentric speakeasy cocktail bar in East Oxford. Or, spend a sophisticated evening watching a jazz recital at one of Oxford's trendy bars; we recommend **Sandy's Piano Bar** for delicious cocktails in an intimate space, or **Oxford Wine Café** for a wine list that will complement the atmosphere perfectly.

CATCH A UNIVERSITY LECTURE

The University of Oxford and **Oxford Brookes University** both host a calendar of public talks, lectures and events throughout the year. Learn something new or brush up on your knowledge and hear from professors that are at the top of their fields.

BOARD GAME CAFÉ

If you're looking for something different, visit the UK's first board game café **Thirsty Meeples**. Open until 10pm, Thirsty Meeples in the perfect way to get sociable (or competitive!) and while away an evening in central Oxford.

1 ▶ *New Theatre*

48 HOURS IN OXFORD
A Whirlwind Weekend

DAY 1
9:30am

Kickstart your weekend in the heart of it all by getting essential information, tickets and advice from the **Oxford Visitor Information Centre** (**♀D3 City**) on Broad Street.

Then, get your bearings by climbing the tower of the **University Church of St Mary the Virgin** for the highest view over Oxford. As you exit the Church, take a stroll around cobbled Radcliffe Square to drink in 360° views of the **Radcliffe Camera**. (**♀E3 City**)

Do you know the best film and literary sites in Oxford?
Read More | p.30 ►

10:45am

To maximise your time, pre-book an **Oxford Official Walking Tour** for a guided walking tour around more of Oxford's iconic sites and locations. Tours are led by accredited guides and usually include entry into one of the **University of Oxford**'s 39 colleges.

Alternatively, if you don't want to walk, the **City Sightseeing** open top bus tour is a great way to see Oxford. Listen to your guide as you are driven around, with the option to hop-on and hop-off at 20 different stops across the city.

1pm
🍴🍷

Allow a little time for shopping and browse the independent shops in the **Covered Market** (**♀ D3 City**). The whole family can choose a picnic for the afternoon; why not try a freshly made sandwich, pastry, pie or even Greek souvlaki?

1 ► *Radcliffe Camera*

2 ► *City Sightseeing*

3 ► *Covered Market*

Whilst in the heart of the city, don't miss Oxford's incredible museums. Choose from the **Ashmolean Museum** (📍 **C2 City**), Britain's first public museum and home to world-famous artefacts and collections, the **History of Science Museum**, the **Museum of Natural History** (📍 **D1 City**) and neighbouring **Pitt Rivers Museum**, the University of Oxford's quirky museum of anthropology and world archaeology.

Alternatively, The **Museum of Oxford** (📍 **D4 City**) tells the history of the city. Best of all... they are all free! Always a city for browsing literature, Oxford's **Blackwell's** bookshop is also worth nipping into.

A wonderfully unique way to spend your time in Oxford, join one of **Bill Spectre's Ghost Trails** on a Friday or Saturday evening. Join Bill, dressed as a Victorian undertaker, as he guides you through the historic city, leaving you with a "deliciously scary tingle down your spine"!

Or, fill your evening with world-class **Choral Evensong** in an Oxford college chapel. These take place every evening during University of Oxford term-time and start between 5:15pm and 6:45pm depending on which college you visit. We recommend joining the Choirs of the grand **Christ Church Cathedral** (📍 **D4 City**) for an unforgettable evening.

Relax in the elegant **Randolph Hotel** (📍 **C2 City**), an icon of Oxford. Enjoy a tipple at the famous Morse Bar in the hotel, before heading to the **Acanthus Restaurant** for outstanding seasonal British cuisine.

Start your day with an exhilarating morning on the water. Take a punt on the river - a truly timeless Oxford tradition - from **Cherwell Boathouse** (read more p.102 ►) to see the city from a different perspective. Alternatively, from Folly Bridge take a chauffeured cruise down the River Thames from **Salter's Steamers**, or **Oxford River Cruises** (📍 **D6 City**) and admire the views of **Christ Church College** in the distance.

Itinerary:
48h in Oxford

2pm

4 ► *Ashmolean Museum*
5&6 ► *Natural History Museum*
7 ► *Bill Spectre*
8 ► *Oxford River Cruises*

6:30pm

9pm

DAY 2
9am

11am 🏰

Take a guided tour of **Oxford Castle & Prison** (📍**C4 City**) and discover the fascinating stories of the building's 1,000-year history. Explore the Saxon St George's Tower and descend deep underground to the 900-year-old crypt.

Noon 🍽️ 🛍️

Close by is **Westgate Oxford** (📍**C4 City**), the city's newest shopping and entertainment centre - and here you will find an eclectic mix of global fashion brands, restaurants, bars and a boutique cinema. Grab lunch with a spectacular view of Oxford's dreaming spires on Westgate's rooftop terrace - we recommend lunching at **Cinnamon Kitchen** for modern Indian cuisine, **Victors** for a touch of modern American small plates, **Pho** for some healthy and hearty Vietnamese street food, or perhaps **The Alchemist** for their theatrical cocktail menu.

1pm

Spend a family-friendly afternoon experiencing the world of children's stories at the newly-transformed **Story Museum**.

For a more grown-up afternoon, treat yourself to an afternoon tour of **The Oxford Artisan Distillery** (📍**F3 City**). One of the world's very few craft distilleries, they use ancient heritage grain to create the finest spirits. Discover the principles and production processes that make their spirits, from their bespoke copper stills to the grain they grow themselves. Finish with a chance to taste their wonderful spirits.

1 ► *Westgate*
2 ► *The Oxford Artisan Distillery*
3 ► *Quod*

3pm 🌿

The Oxford Artisan Distillery's 'Physic Gin' is created using botanicals from **Oxford Botanic Garden** (📍**F4 City**). Wander down from the distillery to the historic Botanic Garden to experience an oasis of green in the city centre. The UK's oldest botanic garden, founded in 1621 as a physic garden growing plants for medicinal research, Oxford Botanic Garden features a formal walled garden, exotic plants in glasshouses and lush herbaceous borders.

7pm

From Oxford Botanic Garden, wander up Oxford's winding High Street, bordered with imposing college walls and independent shops, restaurants and cafes. Opposite University Church and Radcliffe Square you will find **Quod** (📍**E3 City**), a stylish, bustling and contemporary European restaurant perfect for a leisurely dinner in the heart of Oxford.

9pm ⬤

Read more on the nightlife in Oxford p.58 ►

Take a moonlit walk around central Oxford and see the historic University buildings from a different perspective, without the bustle of the city around you. Stroll along the winding lanes often used as shortcuts by students dashing to classes. Stop for a relaxed drink in one of Oxford's sophisticated bars, or settle in for a cosy evening in a historic pub.

EAT

DRINK

SANDERSON

STAY

THE OXFORD CANAL
Oxford to Banbury

Built in the late 18th century to carry commercial barges between Coventry and Oxford, the Oxford Canal is one of the country's most beautiful inland waterways to explore. This route along the towpath takes you through the picturesque scenery of the Cherwell Valley as the canal follows the gentle meandering course of the River Cherwell to Banbury.

Oxford ●

Learn more about
the Cherwell valley
Read More | p.22 ►

Begin your walk along the Oxford Canal from the city centre, following the canal through **Jericho** to the north of the city to enjoy the open views of **Port Meadow.** Cross Port Meadow to enjoy a pint at **The Perch**, a historic thatched pub. At **Upper Wolvercote**, leave the canal towpath to explore the ruins of **Godstow Abbey** and visit **The Trout Inn**, a 17th century pub overlooking the **River Thames** and a favourite of Colin Dexter's **Inspector Morse**.

Thrupp ○
(11km from Oxford)

Continuing north past **Kidlington**, you might want to stop for refreshments at **Thrupp** - a pretty canal side village where rose-covered terraced houses line the towpath and there are two popular pubs, **The Jolly Boatman** and **The Boat Inn**, as well as a tea room. From here the canal follows the winding course of the Cherwell river, joining with it for occasional stretches.

Tackley ○
(7.5km from Thrupp)

Tucked away close to the canal, **Tackley** is a characterful rural village of stone buildings and a church of Saxon origin. Home to a couple of quaint bed and breakfasts, **The Gardiners Arms** pub and a well-stocked village shop with a café, the village makes a good base for exploring the local countryside.

Rousham House ○
(7km from Tackley)

Further north up the canal, the towpath brings you past the grounds of **Rousham House**, a Jacobean country house with wonderful gardens which can be visited. The gardens were landscaped by William Kent in the early 18th century and represent the first phase of English landscape design. Many of the features created in the 18th century are still there today.

At **Lower Heyford Wharf**, Heyford railway station is directly beside the canal, with trains back to Tackley and Oxford or ahead to Banbury. The village of **Lower Heyford** marks approximately the halfway point between Oxford and Banbury and options for an overnight stay include a canal side bed and breakfast as well as **Heyford House** and **The Holt Hotel**. The village's pub, **The Bell**, dates from the 17th century and there is also a café/bistro at Lower Heyford Wharf with gardens overlooking the canal.

Refreshed from a stop in Heyford, continue along the canal as it follows the winding course of the River Cherwell north to **Aynho Wharf**. This is one of the waterway's most appealing stretches as it turns into more open countryside and you will pass the picture-postcard lock-keeper's cottage at **Somerton Deep Lock**. Close to Aynho Wharf is the **Great Western Arms**, a traditional country pub offering bed and breakfast and serving the local **Hook Norton** ales.

From Aynho Wharf continue to **Twyford Wharf** and then the market town of **Banbury** (**♥ C2 County**). In the centre of Banbury an exciting new canal front leisure facility, **Castle Quay Waterfront** - with a cinema, restaurants and a hotel - is being constructed in 2020/21, and it's recommended that you leave the towpath to cross the canal at **The Mill Arts Centre**. Make sure you take a guided tour of the historic **Tooley's Boatyard** which dates from 1788 and is the oldest dry dock working boatyard on the inland waterways.

There are inviting cafes and pubs in the **Old Town**, including the 16th century **Ye Olde Reindeer Inn** where the wood panelled **Globe Room** is believed to have been used by **Oliver Cromwell** as a base during the **Civil War**. Finally, don't leave Banbury without sampling Banbury cakes - delicious spiced and currant-filled pastries which have been made to a secret recipe for over four hundred years!

○ *Lower Heyford*
(0.8km from Rousham)

○ *Aynho*
(16.6km from Lower Heyford)

● *Banbury*
(11km from Aynho)

THE RIVER RAPIDS
Oxford to Henley-on-Thames

The River Rapids is a trio of bus services (X38, X39 & X40) linking Oxford with South Oxfordshire. Here we pick out some of the many things to see and do along the route.

Harcourt Arboretum
(20 mins from Oxford)

The **University of Oxford**'s arboretum is in the small village of **Nuneham Courtenay**. The 130-acre site is open all year round and contains the best collection of trees in **Oxfordshire**, with seasonal highlights including wildflower meadows, rhododendrons and bluebell woods along with plenty of children's activities.

exox.org/venue/harcourt-arboretum

1 to 3 ► *Harcourt Arboretum*
4 ► *Wallingford*
5 ► *Henley*

Dorchester-on-Thames
(8 mins from Harcourt Arboretum)

Stroll around the cute-as-a-doormouse village of **Dorchester-on-Thames**, a village of timber-framed houses. The main attraction in the village is the medieval Abbey, built in the 12th century.

Benson Marina
(7 mins from Dorchester-on-Thames)

A great stop from which to walk along the tranquil banks of the **River Thames** or sit and admire the views of green fields, pretty meadows, farmland and forest from the comfort of the **Waterfront Café**.

Wander the cobbled streets of **Wallingford** (**9 C2 County**) and discover the town's links with both crime novelist **Agatha Christie** and **Midsomer Murders**, as well as the ruins of **Wallingford Castle** and the excellent **Wallingford Museum**.

exox.org/places-to-go/ wallingford

○ *Wallingford*
(10 mins from Benson Marina)

The small village of **Nuffield** is the location of **Nuffield Place**, once home to **William Morris**, founder of the **Morris Motor Company**, and his wife. Their home and personal possessions are just as they left them, the décor and furnishings intact.

○ *Nuffield*
(30 mins from Wallingford)

A picturesque riverside town, home to the famous **Henley Royal Regatta** (1st - 5th July 2020) and the **River and Rowing Museum**. Explore the town on a self-guided walk, browse the independent shops and restaurants or take a stroll along the river.

exox.org/places-to-go/ henley-on-thames

● *Henley-on-Thames*
(**9 E6 County**)
(40 mins from Nuffield)

Learn more about South Oxfordshire
Read More | p.25 ➤

Exploring the River Thames by Bus and Boat

Great for

BY BUS: THAMES TRAVEL

Thames Travel's X38 Oxford to Henley-on-Thames bus service operates every hour Mondays to Saturdays.
The X39 and X40 link Oxford and Wallingford with buses every hour Mondays to Saturdays.

Thames-travel.co.uk/routes/x38x39x40

FAMILIES

HIDDEN GEMS

BY BOAT: SALTER'S STEAMERS

Explore more of the River Thames with Salter's Steamers, with regular public cruises in the summer months between Oxford and Abingdon, Wallingford and Henley, and further south to Reading, Marlowe and Windsor.

exox.org/venue/salters-steamers-boat-trips

NATURE LOVERS

THE RIDGEWAY NATIONAL TRAIL IN OXFORDSHIRE
White Horse Hill to Thame

The Ridgeway Trail stretches 140 kilometres across scenic countryside from Avebury in Wiltshire to Ivinghoe Beacon in Buckinghamshire and through two Areas of Outstanding Natural Beauty: the Chiltern Hills and the North Wessex Downs. This routeway is steeped in history, having been used by traders and invaders as far back as 5,000 years ago. Today it is enjoyed by walkers, cyclists and horse riders seeking far-reaching views, historic sites and wildlife.

White Horse Hill is only 29 kilometres from Oxford, and 20 kilometres away from Watlington. Follow our trail from White Horse Hill to Thame for a taste of how much there is to see and do in this area.

Faringdon ●

Begin in **Faringdon**. The town is full of heritage, immediately noticeable in the quaint town centre where you will find old coaching inns, Georgian fronted buildings and the 17th century town hall. Now occupied by a diverse array of independent shops, cafes and restaurants, the town centre is a hive of activity. A five-minute walk from the town centre, you will find Faringdon's **Folly Tower**. Built in 1935 by Lord Berner, the 100ft high tower sits on a hill amongst a circular woodland, providing panoramic views over the town and beyond.

White Horse Hill and Uffington ○
(10.3km from Faringdon)

Explore The Ridgeway's history at White Horse Hill, where you will find the internationally renowned **Bronze Age White Horse** carved into the chalk hillside. This is the highest point in **Oxfordshire** with views across 6 different counties, and is hugely popular with dog walkers, picnickers and kite fliers alike. There is plenty of parking in the National Trust car park at **White Horse Hill**.

Learn more about the Vale of White Horse Read More | p.27 ➤

From White Horse Hill, walk or ride for 2.3 kilometres along **The Ridgeway** to the prehistoric long barrow of **Wayland's Smithy**. It is also worth venturing off the hills into nearby **Uffington** village (**♀ C5 County**) where there are pubs, a small museum and a waymarked trail to learn more about the historic buildings in the village. There is also the option to camp under the stars near the White Horse at **Britchcombe Farm**.

Base yourself in **Wantage** (♥ **C5 County**) to discover the stories of **King Alfred the Great** who was born in the town in 849AD. This historic market town offers independent shops, places to eat and a theatre, as well as the **Vale and Downland Museum** which has won awards for being family friendly. Head west to villages such as Sparsholt for a nice lunch at **The Star** or **Kingston Lisle** to see the **Blowing Stone** which King Alfred used to summon his army to battle against the Vikings.

Walk up to The Ridgeway to see **Segsbury Camp** hillfort, passing along the chalk stream called the **Letcombe Brook** and through the historic village of **Letcombe Bassett** where you may like to stop for lunch at **The Greyhound** pub. There is also a great day's cycle ride from Wantage eastwards along a signed cycle route through the Lockinges and Ginges and Hendreds villages, then up to The Ridgeway to head westwards back to Wantage. There are some great pubs and historic buildings to look out for in the villages, including a village shop from a bygone age in **East Hendred**!

Goring and **Streatley** is where The Ridgeway meets the River Thames and another **National Trail**, the **Thames Path**. Linked by a bridge in 1837, Streatley and Goring are picturesque riverside villages with numerous places to eat, making this a perfect spot for a break.

From Goring, follow The Ridgeway to walk 8.5 kilometres along the river to the historic market town of **Wallingford** (♥ **D5 County**), with independent shops, places to eat and stay and a small museum. Families will enjoy Wallingford's riverside playground and campsite.

○ *Wantage*
(14km from White
Horse Hill along
Ridgeway
Bus links to Oxford:
Stagecoach
S8 or S9)

1 ➤ *Faringdon Folly*
2 ➤ *Wantage Market*
3 ➤ *King Alfred*

○ *Streatley Goring*
(24km from Wantage
along The Ridgeway)

○ *Wallingford*
(10.6km from Goring)

Watlington
(17.7km from
Wallingford *)*

From Wallingford, there is a scenic day's walk along The Ridgeway to the attractive historic town of **Watlington**. This area is known as the **Chiltern Hills**, famous for its parklands and beechwoods. The first stretch passes along **Grim's Ditch,** a ditch and bank boundary thought to date back to Saxon times. Watlington is where a huge hoard of Viking coins was famously found in 2016. Some of these coins displayed the head of King Alfred the Great and a replica display can be seen in Watlington's library.

Lewknor M40
Coach stop
(17km from
Watlington
Coaches to London,
Oxford, Heathrow
and Gatwick)
Thame
Thame train
station

Finish your journey in the thriving market town of **Thame** (♦ **E4 County**), perfectly situated at the foot of the Chiltern Hills, just 23 kilometres from Oxford. From historic buildings to beautiful parks, the **Thame Museum**, **The Players Theatre**, and a vibrant **High Street** - Thame has lots of exciting attractions and activities to enjoy.

Great for

NATURE LOVERS

HISTORY

ADVENTURERS

Baggage transfer

1 ➤ *Wallingford*
2 ➤ *Thame Town*
Hall

If you want to walk or ride along the Trail without the weight of baggage, there are baggage handling companies and accommodation providers who can take your bags to your next stop. See the National Trails website for details.

For more information on car parking, taxis and train stations, please visit nationaltrail.co.uk/ridgeway.

PLAN YOUR NEXT BUS TRIP. EASY.

Get around Oxfordshire by bus, with the Stagecoach Bus App.

- Mobile tickets
- Interactive map to track your bus
- Clear bus times with expected arrivals
- Simple journey planning

Download the Stagecoach Bus App

stagecoachbus.com

EXPLORE THE COTSWOLDS
Woodstock to Burford

It's easy to see more of Oxfordshire using public transport. Follow the route of the Stagecoach 233 service linking Woodstock to Witney and Burford to discover many fascinating places along the way. The bus runs roughly every 20 minutes Monday to Saturday.

Woodstock
Blenheim Palace

Start your journey in the historic town of **Woodstock** (**♥ C3 County**), home to **The Oxfordshire Museum** and **Soldiers of Oxfordshire Museum**, as well as antique shops, great pubs, and the 13th century **Macdonald Bear Hotel**. No visit to Woodstock would be complete without a visit to **Blenheim Palace** (**♥ C3 County**), a **UNESCO World Heritage Site** and birthplace of **Winston Churchill**.

Long Hanborough
(11 mins from Woodstock)

A few minutes further is **Long Hanborough** train station. The station is on the **Great Western Railway** line linking **London Paddington** to the **Cotswolds**, and close by are the **Oxford Bus Museum** and **Morris Motors Museum**. Both tell the story of transport in **Oxford**, including the production of cars by **Morris Motors**.

North Leigh
(1 hour walk from Long Hanborough)

Further along is **North Leigh Roman Villa**, one of the largest villas from Roman Britain set on the banks of the **River Evenlode**. It's a 2.5 kilometre walk from the bus stop on the main road, but worth the pretty walk to see a near complete mosaic tile floor dating back to the 3rd century.

Witney
(30 mins from Long Hanborough)

Jump back on the bus and the next stop is the old market town of **Witney** (**♥ C4 County**). The town is home to **Cogges Manor Farm**, where visitors can feed the pygmy goats, play in the adventure park, or learn about the history of the 13th century manor house. For ale lovers, discover **Wychwood Brewery**; join one of the brewery's tour experiences to learn how their award-winning Wychwood beers are crafted.

From Witney, your journey will take you through the picturesque village of **Minster Lovell**. Explore the riverside ruins of 15th century **Minster Lovell Hall**. Stop at the charming **Old Swan** or **Minster Mill** hotels for a delicious meal or relaxing overnight stay.

○ *Minster Lovell*
(7 mins from Witney)

Learn more about
West Oxfordshire
Read More | p.29 ➤

Another 8 kilometres from Minster Lovell, leave the bus in **Shilton**. Nearby is **Crocodiles of the World**, the UK's only crocodile zoo, and **Cotswold Wildlife Park and Gardens** (📍**B4 County**), where visitors can discover more than 250 species of animal, including rhinos, lemurs and penguins.

○ *Shilton*
(18 mins from
Minster Lovell)

Finally, the route stops in **Burford** (📍**B4 County**), frequently referred to as the 'gateway to the Cotswolds'. Home to rows of idyllic honey stone cottages, tea shops and boutiques, Burford is a place full of character and Cotswold charm.

● *Burford*
(10 mins from
Shilton)

1 ➤ *Blenheim Palace*
2&3 ➤ *Witney*
4&5 ➤ *Minster Mill*
6 ➤ *Cotswold*
Wildlife Park
7 ➤ *Burford*

Great for

FAMILIES

HISTORY

NATURE LOVERS

ACROSS THE COTSWOLDS
Oxford to Worcester

Spanning four counties, Great Western Railway's Cotswold Line journeys past the dramatic Malvern Hills and through the orchards of the Vale of Evesham, running alongside the River Evenlode, via pretty towns and quaint villages of honey-coloured stone, charming churches and country pubs.

Oxford

Depart from **Oxford**, having seen the colleges, castle and culture of the city. A delightful train journey across rolling countryside is the perfect way to see more of England from your base in Oxford.

Long Hanborough
(10 mins from Oxford)

Your first stop is **Long Hanborough** train station (**♀ C4 County**). Close by is the **Oxford Bus Museum** and **Morris Motors Museum**. The Museum houses vintage buses, coaches, bicycles, and even a horse tram - telling the story of Oxfordshire's transport history, including the production of cars by Morris Motors.

Charlbury
(7 mins from Long Hanborough)

From Hanborough the line enters the **Cotswold Area of Outstanding Natural Beauty**. **Charlbury**, once a clearing in the **Wychwood Forest** and now an idyllic market town, lends itself to gentle strolls past historic buildings and colourful cottage gardens. Cornbury Park near Charlbury is home to the **Cornbury** and **Wilderness Festivals** each year.

Kingham
(9 mins from Charlbury)

Kingham is a peaceful village, surrounded by the rolling hills of Cotswold countryside and offering a true taste of rural Cotswold life. Hole up in **The Wild Rabbit**, a top foodie destination, before grabbing some fresh air - Kingham is an excellent centre for walking and cycling. Then, make some four-legged friends at nearby **Cotswold Farm Park**, run by *Countryfile's* Adam Henson.

From Kingham, your journey will take you beyond the borders of Oxfordshire to the picturesque town of **Moreton-in-Marsh**, which dates back 1000 years to the Saxon era. Explore Moreton's elegant High Street which houses antique emporiums, galleries and tea rooms. Stop for a break at a pub or restaurant, including one said to be the inspiration for The Prancing Pony in JRR Tolkien's *Lord of the Rings*.

Nearby is **Batsford Arboretum**, the country's largest private collection of trees and shrubs. Wander through 56 acres of wild gardens and marvel at stunning views across the **Evenlode Valley**.

While you're in Moreton-in-Marsh, why not join a tour to discover more of the Cotswolds with **Go Cotswolds** (read more p.92 ➤)or **Fowler Tours** (read more p.99 ➤)?

Hop off the train at **Evesham**, a historic riverside market town nestled in the **Vale of Evesham** - the "fruit and vegetable basket of England". So much fruit grows around Evesham that the town hosts a famous Blossom Trail every April/May, which leads across 40 miles of pretty countryside. To soak up some culture, visit the **Almonry Museum** or the art-deco **Regal Cinema**.

Finally, finish your journey in **Worcester**. One of the oldest cities in the country, Worcester is famed for its magnificent Cathedral, fascinating Civil War history and world-renowned industrial past... and **Worcestershire Sauce**. Head to the bank of the **River Severn** for great views of the Cathedral and city from a different perspective.

Itinerary:
Across the
Cotswolds

○ *Moreton-in-Marsh*
(7 mins from Kingham)

○ *Evesham*
(17 mins from Moreton-in-Marsh)

● *Worcester Foregate Street*
(30 mins from Evesham)

Transport

Great Western Railway's Cotswold Line runs from London Paddington via Oxford to Worcester or Hereford. Trains leave Oxford roughly every hour.

Detailed timetable information is available at gwr.com.

For journeys within Oxfordshire and the Cotswolds, Great Western Railways' '*Cotswolds Discoverer*' tickets offer great value. **gwr.com/discover.**

1 ➤ *Oxford Bus Museum*
2 ➤ *Chastleton House*
3 ➤ *Batsford Arboretum*
4 ➤ *Bibury - Arlington Row*
credit: Go Cotswolds

EASY DAY TRIPS
from Oxford

As one of the most centrally located cities in England, Oxford is the perfect place to base yourself to explore other parts of the country. Excellent transport links makes it easy to travel around Oxfordshire and beyond.

Drive time:
1 hour 20 minutes

Transport:
Book a tour from Gulliver's Guides or International Friends at Oxford Visitor Information Centre
01865 686446

STONEHENGE

Walk in the footsteps of your Neolithic ancestors at Stonehenge (**♀ C6 County (further south)**) - one of the wonders of the world and the best-known prehistoric monument in Europe. Travelling by train to **Salisbury** takes just over two hours, and the journey time to drive by car is just over one hour, giving you plenty of time to explore this wonderful English Heritage site. You can even purchase discount tickets for Stonehenge from the **Oxford Visitor Information Centre**.

Take a day trip on the train from Oxford to Worcester across the Cotswolds
Read More | p.76 ➤

Drive time:
1 hour 30 minutes

Transport:
GWR train,
1 hour 20 minutes

BATH

With frequent services on the rail route between Oxford and Bath (**♀ A6 County**) taking just over one hour, the beautiful city of Bath is the perfect day trip destination. Built for pleasure and relaxation, Bath has been a wellbeing destination since Roman times, boasting the only natural thermal hot springs in Britain you can bathe in.

BLETCHLEY PARK

Once the top-secret home of World War II codebreakers and the birthplace of modern information technology, Bletchley Park (**♀F2 County**) is now a vibrant heritage attraction. Just a fifty-minute drive away, this is a great day trip to take from Oxford, allowing you to take your time to immerse yourself in this fascinating piece of British heritage, and still have time to enjoy a full evening's entertainment back in Oxford.

Drive time:
1 hour

Transport:
Stagecoach X5
bus from Oxford to
Milton Keynes

STRATFORD-UPON-AVON

Nestled in the rural **Warwickshire** countryside, on the picturesque banks of the **River Avon**, lies the charming medieval market town of Stratford-upon-Avon (**♀ B1 County**). A day trip to the birthplace of **William Shakespeare**, the world's greatest playwright, is a must and it's so easy to get there either by bus, with a journey time of just over an hour, or by train via **Royal Leamington Spa**.

Drive time:
1 hour

Transport:
GWR train
to Evesham,
Stagecoach X18 bus
to Stratford-upon-
Avon

LONDON

Less than an hour's journey via train from Oxford, London's lively city (**♀ F5 County**) atmosphere is not to be missed. Take in a show in the West End, stroll around the UK's most famous museums, and marvel at some of the grandest monuments in Europe.

Drive time:
1 hour 30 minutes

Transport:
GWR and Chiltern
Railway trains,
approx. 1 hour.
Oxford Tube coach,
approx. 2 hours

Fly to over 450 destinations worldwide

Whether it's a city break in **Europe**, exploring the outback in **Australia**, experiencing the sights of **Asia** or travelling to **America**, we can get you there.

With 35 airline partners to choose from, it's time to start your adventure at **Birmingham Airport**.

birminghamairport.co.uk

Here for **your journey**

GETTING TO
Oxfordshire

BY AIR

Nearest airports: **London Heathrow Airport** (1.5 hours by bus), **London Gatwick Airport** (2 hours by bus), **Birmingham Airport** (1 hour by train). **Oxford Bus Company Airline** coaches operate 24 hour, 7 days a week services to both Heathrow and Gatwick airports. Tickets can be purchased online or on the day of travel.
Airline.oxfordbus.co.uk
GWR and Chiltern Railways both provide rail tickets between Birmingham International and Oxford.

BY COACH

Linking London and Oxford, **Stagecoach** operates the **Oxford Tube** which provides a 24/7 service.
Oxfordtube.com

BY RAIL

Great Western Railway has a regular service from **London Paddington** stopping at Didcot, Reading and Oxford and north through the county to the Cotswolds.
Gwr.com
Chiltern Railways operates trains from **London Marylebone** with stops at Princes Risborough, Haddenham & Thame Parkways, Bicester Village, Oxford Parkway and Oxford.
Chilternrailways.co.uk

1 ► *Birmingham Airport*
2 ► *Great Western Railway*

TRAVELLING AROUND
Oxfordshire

BY BUS

The **Oxford Bus Company** operates a network of services across the city, with regular buses also travelling to surrounding towns and villages as well as to **Blenheim Palace** (♥ C2 County).
Oxfordbus.co.uk

Stagecoach also offers an excellent countryside bus network, including the S5 service linking Oxford and **Bicester Village** (♥ D3 County), and the S3 and S7 services linking **Oxford** and **Blenheim Palace** (♥C2 County).
Stagecoachbus.com/about/Oxfordshire

Park & Ride - The Gateway to Oxford. There are 5 **Park & Ride** sites located around Oxford's ring road, with regular bus services to the city centre, making your journey into the city hassle-free.
Parkandride.oxfordbus.co.uk

The **City Sightseeing Bus** is an excellent way to explore the city, its history and highlights, and offers the option to hop on and off whenever you like. Tickets are valid for 24 to 48 hours.
Citysightseeingoxford.com

BY TRAIN

Explore West Oxfordshire via the **GWR Cotswolds Line** (see itinerary p.68 ►) or North Oxfordshire via the GWR **Oxford Canal Line** (see itinerary on p.54 ►). To discover South Oxfordshire, catch the **GWR** train to Paddington and alight at Didcot Parkway for local transport options.

CAR HIRE AND TAXIS

Oxford Carriage Company offer a range of private transport services from airport transfers to long distance travel and day trips.
Oxfordcarriage.co.uk

Royal Cars offer taxi services in Oxford, and offer transport from local runs to airport transfers and long-distance journeys.
Royal-cars.com

Townhouse Executive Travel & Tours offers luxury travel in their fleet of Mercedes cars for both local and long-distance transfers including airports and stations.
Townhousewoodstock.co.uk

Auto Europe offer car, motorhome, motorcycle or luxury vehicle hire from a choice of suppliers to suit your needs.
Autoeurope.co.uk

Chauffeur / Guide hire
Concierge History Tours offer luxury tour and chauffeur hire in either a Rolls Royce or a Bentley.
Conciergehistorytours.co.uk

Vintage Days Out combine chauffeur-driven vintage Rolls Royces with private cruises in vintage boats along the River Thames.
Vintagedaysout.com

Gullivers Guides offer transport and a guided tour in one, running tours across Oxford and Oxfordshire and beyond.
Gulliversguides.co.uk

The Oxford Minibus Company has a high-end fleet of minibuses catering for 1-70 passengers.
Theoxfordminibuscompany.co.uk

BY BOAT

Hire a narrowboat to explore the length of the county from a different perspective. Travel along the River Thames, River Cherwell or Oxford Canal. Or, take a river cruise with **Oxford River Cruises** or **Salters Steamers**.

ON FOOT

Oxford city centre is entirely walkable - and we recommend you explore by foot to see the most of the city! If you're finding your bearings, **Oxford Official Walking Tours** offer award-winning tours of the city. There are plenty of stunning countryside walks across Oxfordshire, including the **Ridgeway Trail** (see itinerary p.62 ➤) or **Thames Path**.

BY BIKE

Oxford is a fairly flat city, and perfect for exploring by bike. **Bainton Bikes** operate across Oxford, and offer different styles of bike to hire according to your needs. To explore the surrounding county by bicycle, why not arrange a self-guided cycle tour with **Active England Tours**?

·T·R·A·V·E·L·
FREE
RANGE

Hop on board a Chiltern Railways train to Oxford from lovely London Marylebone. Enjoy your journey with spacious carriages, comfy seats and complimentary Wifi*. With trains leaving twice an hour, with journey times from just 60 minutes, isn't it time you spread your wings?

Book online now or tap the app

Chilternrailways
by arriva

* Subject to availability

OXFORDSHIRE
for your Clients

As well as being a world-class leisure destination, Oxfordshire is a fantastic place to meet and do business. Where else could you hold your meeting in a room that was once home to **Oscar Wilde** or dine where **C S Lewis**, **William Gladstone** and **Rowan Atkinson** regularly ate, then let your delegates spend the evening networking on the banks of the Thames?

From UNESCO world-heritage palaces and ancient libraries, to high tech venues & cutting-edge research, Oxfordshire is home to a diverse range of venues suitable for everything from biotech conventions, to luxury incentive breaks, to corporate retreats – all within close proximity (just an hour) of **London**.

If you work in the business events sector, we have a dedicated team to help you develop itineraries and conferences for your clients.

The **Experience Oxfordshire Venues Service** is the official and free conference and event venue-finding bureau for Oxford and Oxfordshire. The team will match your brief to one or more venues in the historic heart of academic Oxford or the surrounding countryside, completely free of charge. We have helped hundreds of event organisers create successful events in Oxford and Oxfordshire and we would love to assist you too.

If you work in the travel trade, please get in touch with the **Experience Oxfordshire** team, who will be happy to recommend inspiring itinerary ideas, venues and products, including the new **Oxford Pass**.

We look forward to welcoming your clients to our world-class destination very soon.

experienceoxfordshire.org/venues
@ExOxVenues

1 ► *Heythrop Park Resort*

2 ► *New College Garden*
credit: Sarah Rhodes

3 ► *Belmond Le Manoir Aux Quat Saisons*

Where to Stay

See City map (p.12-13)
and County map (p54-55)

 Child Friendly   **WiFi**   **Disabled Friendly**   **Parking Included**   **Animal Friendly**   **Food/Bar**

THE OLD PARSONAGE | ♀ C1 City

Best known for its eclectic country house charm, chic modern interiors and striking 20th century portraits, the hotel is a luxury five star home-from-home with impeccable hospitality. Five Star - Meeting Rooms

🖥 www.oldparsonagehotel.co.uk 📞 01865 292305 OX2 6NN

THE FEATHERED NEST COUNTRY INN | ♀ B3 County

Traditional inn with upscale dining, open fire and relaxed bar.
From £210 B&B for a Double Room
3 AA Rosette Stars

01993 833030 · OX7 6SD · www.thefeatherednestinn.co.uk

HOLIDAY INN OXFORD | ♀ C1 City (Further North)

Contemporary rooms, free parking, located close to city centre.
From £66 for a Double Room

08719 429086 · OX2 8JD · www.holidayinn.com/oxford

BATH PLACE HOTEL | ♀ E3 City

Bath Place is a cluster of 17th century cottages in Oxford.
From £140 B&B for a Double Room
Three Star

01865 791812 · OX1 3SU · www.bathplace.co.uk

BICESTER HOTEL AND SPA | ♀ D3 County

Four-star resort set among acres of beautiful countryside. **From £99 for a Classic Room**
Four Star - Spa - Health Club - Performance Gym - Outdoor Swimming Lake - Golf Course - Lounge

01869 241204 · OX26 1TH · www.bicesterhotelgolfandspa.com

HAMPTON BY HILTON OXFORD | ♀ E6 City (Further South)

Modern, stylish accommodation at affordable prices. Included for all guests are free parking, free breakfast and free wifi. **From £75 B&B for a Double Room.** Breakfast included - Use of fitness room included.

01865 788860 · OX4 4XP
www.hilton.com/en/hotels/oxfhxhx-hampton-oxford

EGROVE PARK, SAÏD BUSINESS SCHOOL | ♀ A6 City (Further South-East)

Egrove Park is located in a stunning setting 2 miles from Oxford.
From £86 for a Double Room

01865 288800 · OX5 1NZ
www.sbs.ox.ac.uk/about-us/venue-hire/bb-accommodation

THE OLD SCHOOL BED AND BREAKFAST | ♀ B2 County

Award winning home from home in the North Cotswolds. **From £142 for a Double Room.**
Five Star - Walkers - Cyclists - Breakfast - 5 Star Gold VisitEngland Award - Afternoon tea & homemade cake included.

01608 674588 · GL56 0SL · www.theoldschoolbedandbreakfast.com

---

HAWKWELL HOUSE HOTEL | ♀ E6 City (Further South)

Private gardens, historical character and contemporary designs. **From £88 for a Double Room** 24-Hour Reception - Luggage Store - Iron/ Ironing Board - Private Dining

01865 749988 · OX4 4DZ · www.hawkwellhouse.co.uk

MACDONALD BEAR HOTEL | 9 C3 County

📞 01993 811124   ⊙ Park Street, Woodstock, OX20 1SZ
💻 www.macdonaldhotels.co.uk/our-hotels/south-england/
woodstock/macdonald-bear-hotel

Macdonald Bear Hotel is one of the finest hotels in Oxfordshire and offers a beautiful slice of luxury in the heart of the countryside. Set in Woodstock, in what was once a 13th century coaching inn, their hotel combines history and culture with exceptional facilities. The Bear Hotel boasts delicious food at its best. Savour classic British dishes and delicious afternoon tea with a modern twist and fine wines at the award-winning restaurant headed by Chef James Mearing right in the heart of Oxfordshire. Only the finest British cuisine made with local, organic vegetables and dairy products.

From £160 B&B for a Double Room - Four Star - Two AA Rosette Restaurant

🍽 🛜 👥 🐾

HEYTHROP PARK RESORT | 9 C3 County

📞 01608 673333   💻 www.heythroppark.co.uk   ⊙ Heythrop Park Resort, Enstone, Chipping Norton, OX7 5UF

Nestled in 440 acres of stunning countryside on the edge of the Cotswolds, 4* Heythrop Park Resort is one of the most impressive hotels around Oxford with both age-old decadence and contemporary style - incorporating an 18th-century manor house and a stylish, modern part of the estate, creating limitless opportunities for business, and the perfect setting for leisure breaks, weddings and lots more!

Heythrop Park Resort has complimentary car parking on-site, free Wi-Fi, 358 bedrooms over the resort, a state-of-the-art seated tiered auditorium seating up to 400, a permanent marquee catering up to 800, a ballroom for a capacity of up to 350, 29 meeting rooms over the resort, an 18 hole championship golf course, health & leisure club, Footgolf course, spa, restaurant and bar.

Whether you're looking for a sublime setting for an afternoon tea, a memorable dining room for a private dinner, an impressive large space to host a corporate gala dinner, a magical setting for an exclusive wedding or a seasonal escape in the countryside; they have something for everyone! Want to know more? Make an appointment with their team, they'd be delighted to show you around and discuss your requirements.

Four Star - Meeting Rooms - Golf Course - Spa - Leisure Club

🍽

GRANGE FARM COUNTRY COTTAGES

📍 **D5 County**

📞 **07919 002132** 💻 **www.grangefarmcottages.co.uk**
 Grange Farm Country Estate, Godington, Bicester OX27 9AF

Gold Award winning, 4-star self-catering cottages set on a beautiful, peaceful family farm. Based in rural Oxfordshire, but with easy access to the Cotswolds, Blenheim Palace, Stowe, Bicester Village and Oxford. Our cottages are all fitted out with contemporary practical items, character furnishings and offer a range of accommodation options. Kitchen areas have a full-sized cooker, fridge, microwave oven and dishwasher. Fishing lake on site and countryside walks.

Dogs welcome. Come and meet their family horses and alpacas! Open all year round. Four Star

🅿 📶 👫 🐾

JURYS INN OXFORD HOTEL AND CONFERENCE VENUE

📍 **C1 City**
(Further North)

📞 **01865 489988** 💻 **www.jurysinns.com/hotels/oxford**
 Godstow Road, Oxford, OX2 8AL

Welcome to Jurys Inn Oxford Hotel and Conference Venue. Step inside their 240-bedroom hotel just a short drive from the city centre. Their four-star Oxford hotel is the perfect base for adventures in and around Oxford's fascinating historic city, whether you're staying for one night or an entire week. Their hotel also features one of the most celebrated restaurants, Marco Pierre White's Steakhouse, Bar and Grill. The restaurant combines British and French influences to serve up perfectly-cooked dishes and hand-crafted cocktails.
From £85 for a Double Room Four Star

🅿 📶

MALMAISON OXFORD

📍 **C4 City**

📞 **01865 689944**   **www.malmaison.com/locations/oxford**
💻 **3 New Road, Oxford Castle Quarter, Oxford, OX1 1AY**

Malmaison Oxford, a boutique hotel located in the Castle Quarter. Comprising of 95 rooms and suites and housed in a former prison, their bedrooms are rather more spacious than your average jail cell. Enjoy sumptuous dining in their stylish Brasserie, where fresh, local and classic dishes are cooked to perfection. Be sure to stop by their neon-lit bar, where the only clink is the sound of glasses as you raise a toast with cocktails, world-class wines or refreshing beers. This is without a doubt one of the most unique hotels in Oxford city centre. So who wants to escape? It would be a crime not to.
From £129 for a Double Room

📶

BEST WESTERN PLUS LINTON LODGE HOTEL
9 C1 City (Further North)

📞 01865 553461   💻 www.bw-lintonlodgehotel.co.uk
📍 1-13 Linton Road, Oxford, OX2 6UJ

Perfect location for Oxford and the Cotswolds.... Previously an Edwardian house still with some original features but fully converted, the hotel is set in 1.5 acres of tranquil gardens, in a leafy suburb just a mile from the city centre of Oxford. A fusion of Edwardian and Contemporary, with a direct route to Bicester Village Outlet Shopping Centre. Situated just off Banbury Road where there are buses to the city centre every few minutes or a leisurely 20 minute stroll passing many notable landmarks along the way.

From £85 for a Double Room

🅿 📶

COURTYARD BY MARRIOTT OXFORD SOUTH
9 D5 County

New modern 4* hotel with award-winning Oxen Bar & Grill. 170 bedrooms with all mod cons and rainfall showers. Free parking and WiFi and easy access into Oxford via the A34 in 25 minutes. **From £110 for a Double Room.** Four Star

🅿 📶 ♿ 👪

💻 www.marriott.co.uk/hotels/travel/oxfcx-courtyard-oxford-south
📞 01865 671480   😊 OX14 4FP

HOLIDAY INN EXPRESS OXFORD
9 E6 City (Further South)

Fully refurbished, air conditioning in all rooms, comfy beds, power showers, reception staffed 24 hours. Breakfast & WiFi included in rate, free parking. Three restaurants within 4 minutes walking distance. **From £79 for a Standard Room.** Park Leisure Pool & Gym special rates for hotel guests.

🅿 📶 ♿ 👪

💻 www.holidayinnexpress.com   📞 01865 780888   😊 OX4 4XP

EYNSHAM HALL
9 C4 County

A unique Grade II listed mansion set within a 47-acre country estate. 52 stylish bedrooms - Health & Fitness Club - Fine, locally sourced, seasonal food - Award-winning - Gun Room - Three Star

🍽 🅿 📶 ♿ 👪 🐾

💻 www.eynshamhall.com   📞 01993 885200   😊 OX29 6PN

THE OLD BANK
9 E3 City

Central 5-star hotel with 43 luxury bedrooms, many with unrivalled views of the city's most famous landmarks... Quod Restaurant & Bar forms the lively hub of the Old Bank Hotel. Five Star - Meeting Rooms

🍽 🅿 📶 ♿ 👪

💻 www.oldbankhotel.co.uk   📞 01865 799599   😊 OX1 4BJ

BELMOND LE MANOIR AUX QUAT'SAISONS | 📍 E4 County

📞 01844 278881 ⊙ Church Road, Great Milton, Oxford, OX44 7PD

💻 www.belmond.com/hotels/europe/uk/oxfordshire/belmond-le-manoir-aux-quat-saisons

Created by celebrated chef Raymond Blanc OBE, Belmond Le Manoir aux Quat'Saisons is one of the country's most cherished manor house hotels. They received two Michelin stars in 1984, the first year of their opening, and, remarkably, have held them ever since.

Surrounded by lawns, flower borders and orchards, their setting is postcard-perfect. But beyond the eye-catching displays are vegetable and herb gardens that provide the kitchen—and the acclaimed Raymond Blanc Cookery School—with ultra-fresh, organic produce. They guarantee their restaurant remains at the cutting edge of culinary excellence. **Prices start from £695 based on a Deluxe bedroom and includes breakfast.** Five Star 🍽 🅿 🛜 ♿ 👥 🐾

THE CHEQUERS AT BURCOT | 📍 D5 County

The Chequers at Burcot has 9 contemporary boutique rooms decorated and appointed with all modern amenities along with an award-winning restaurant and pub. The perfect base to explore Oxfordshire from.

🅿 🛜 ♿ 👥

💻 www.thechequers-burcot.co.uk 📞 01865 407771 ⊙ OX14 3DP

THE RANDOLPH HOTEL | 📍 C2 City

The Randolph Hotel offers luxury bedrooms, tranquil spa and world-class dining. It's the perfect setting for comfort and indulgence in the heart of Oxford. Five Star

🍽 🅿 🛜 ♿ 👥

💻 www.randolphhotel.co.uk 📞 0344 8799132 ⊙ OX1 2LN

VOCO OXFORD THAMES HOTEL | 📍 E6 City (Further South)

Riverside hotel, 30 acres of beautiful grounds and gardens, free parking.
From £150 B&B.
Four Star
🅿 🛜 ♿ 👥 🐾

01865 334444 · OX4 4GX · www.oxfordthames.vocohotels.com

ABODES BED & BREAKFAST | 📍 E6 City (Further South)

Nice and affordable B&B providing a great home-from-home welcome.
From £50 B&B for a Double Room.
Four Star - Federation of Small Business
🅿 🛜

07590 347898 · OX1 5NU · www.bnboxford.co.uk

ARDEN LODGE | 📍 C1 City (Further North)

A cosy three-star guest house in a quiet suburb of Oxford.
From £60 B&B for a Double Room
Three Star
🅿 🛜 ♿ 👥 🐾

01865 552076 · OX2 8DX · www.ardenlodgeoxford.co.uk

MERCURE OXFORD EASTGATE HOTEL | 📍 F4 City

17th-century coaching-inn, central location and modern rooms.
Four Star
🍽 🅿 🛜 ♿ 👥

01865 248332 · OX1 4BE · www.accorhotels.com

STAYCOTSWOLD 01993 259 444   www.staycotswold.com   OX18 4XH   📍 B4 County

DOUBLE TREE BY HILTON OXFORD BELFRY   01844 279381   OX9 2JW   📍 E4 County

GORSELANDS HALL   01993 882292   www.gorselandshall.com   OX29 6PU   📍 C4 County

MINSTER MILL   01993 774441   www.minstermill.co.uk   OX29 0RN   📍 C4 County

THE BUTTERY   01865 811950   www.thebutteryhotel.co.uk   OX1 3AP   📍 D3 City

OXFORD SPIRES HOTEL   01865 324324   www.oxfordspireshotel.co.uk   OX1 4PS   📍 D6 City

ROYAL OXFORD HOTEL   01865 248432   www.royaloxfordhotel.co.uk   OX11 1HR   📍 B3 City

LITTLEGOOD LODGE   01295 750069   www.littlegoodfarm.co.uk   OX17 1QZ   📍 C2 County

THE BURLINGTON HOUSE   01865 513513   www.burlington-hotel-oxford.co.uk   OX2 7PP   📍 C1 City (Further North)

THE GALAXIE   01865 515688   www.galaxie.co.uk   OX2 7BY   📍 C1 City (Further North)

THE ARTIST RESIDENCE   01993 656220   www.artistresidence.co.uk/our-hotels/oxford   OX29 6XN   📍 C4 County

ST. MARGARETS HOTEL   01865 433864   www.thestmargaretshotel.co.uk   OX2 6LD   📍 C1 City (Further North)

OLD SWAN   01993 862512   www.oldswan.co.uk   OX29 0RN   📍 C4 County

CHRIST CHURCH   01865 276492   www.chch.ox.ac.uk/conferences/staying-christ-church   OX1 1DP   📍 D4 City

THE GEORGE HOTEL   01491 836665   www.peelhotels.co.uk/george-hotel   OX10 0BS   📍 D5 County

OXFORD BROOKES, SCOTT HOUSE   01865 488400   www.brookes.ac.uk/venues/accommodation/scott-house   OX2 9AT   📍 A4 City (Further West)

For Your Event

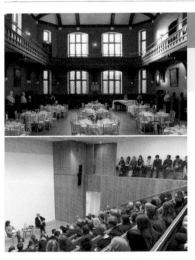
OXFORD FINE DINING EVENT CATERERS   01865 728240   www.oxfordfinedining.co.uk   OX25 3QW

91

What to See and Do

ALICE'S SHOP - THE ALICE IN WONDERLAND SHOP   01865 240338   www.aliceinwonderlandshop.com   OX1 1RA   **♀ D5 City**

THE TURRILL SCULPTURE GARDEN   07922 205946   www.turrillsculpturegarden.org.uk   OX2 7JL   **♀ C1 City** (Further North)

MINI PLANT OXFORD FACTORY TOURS   01865 824387   www.visit-mini.com   OX4 6NL   **♀ D4 County**

ST MICHAEL AT THE NORTH GATE   01865 240940   www.smng.org.uk/wp   OX1 3EY   **♀ D3 City**

COGGES MANOR FARM | **♀ C4 County**

Cogges is a unique historic farm, made famous as Yew Tree Farm in Downton Abbey. Visit to explore the beautiful manor house, stunning walled garden, unspoilt grounds, and meet their friendly animals.
Adults £6.50 | Children £4.50 | Family: £19.50

🖥 www.cogges.org.uk   📞 01993 772602   ⊚ OX28 3LA

OXFORD CASTLE AND PRISON | **♀ C4 City**

📞 01865 260663   🖥 www.oxfordcastleandprison.co.uk   ⊚ 44-46 Oxford Castle, Oxford, OX1 1AY

Explore the 1 000-year history of Oxford Castle & Prison. Step back in time with their costumed guided tours and see fascinating stories come to life. Hear the great tales of Empress Matilda, the fate of Mary Blandy and step inside their padded jail cell.

Find gorgeous views atop of St. Georges' Tower and then descend into the atmospheric crypt of St. Georges' Chapel. Here you can touch the stones where Oxford University was rumoured to begin and stand in the birthplace of Geoffrey of Monmouth's *Legend of King Arthur*. Wander the austere confines of the prison's D-Wing and debtors tower and learn about their youngest inmates.
After your guided tour, you can explore the prison cells at your own leisure and dress up like a prisoner in their exhibition space. Head outside and climb the mound, the remains of their motte and bailey castle.

In the summer, they host Knight School, a medieval inspired workshop that trains children into becoming little warriors. Their Shakespeare Festival is an Oxford summer staple whilst Ghost Fest is sure to give you a scare over Halloween.

They open from 10am - 4.20pm daily. Guided tours up to every 20 minutes. The guided tour lasts approximately 1 hour.

Open Daily 10am - 5:30pm (last tour 4:20pm)
Adults £12.95 | Children £8.75 | Seniors £11.95 | Students £11.95

HOOK NORTON BREWERY | C2 County

📞 01608 730384 🖥 www.hooky.co.uk
☺ Brewery Lane, Hook Norton, Banbury, OX15 5NY

Come and experience the sights and sounds of brewing unchanged in over 6 generations. Hook Norton Brewery run tours of their 5-storey Victorian Tower Brewery 7 days a week and have an on-site cafe and shop along with a free brewery and village museum. Their shire horse team, which they still use to deliver beer, can be found in the stables and they run the original steam engine on the first Saturday of each month. The Brewery also have rooms available for private hire, parties, meetings and weddings. Alongside that they also brew a wide range of award-winning cask ales, keg beers and lager.

(Brewery Tour) Adults £15 | Concessions £12.50

SALTERS STEAMERS | D6 City

Salters Steamers is a family run passenger boat business operating for over 160 years. They offer self drive hire boats, punts and skiffs. They also operate 40 minute trips to Iffley lock - please see website.

🖥 www.salterssteamers.co.uk 📞 01865 243421 ☺ OX1 4LA

BOMBAY SAPPHIRE DISTILLERY | D6 County

Located in Hampshire, 45 minutes from Oxford, the distillery is home to all the world's Bombay Sapphire gin. Book using promo code Oxford20 for 20% off the Discovery tour - valid until 31st March 2020.
Adult £17.50 | Child aged 0-5 FREE | Child aged 6-17 £10.00 | Concession £15.75

🖥 www.distillery.bombaysapphire.com 📞 01256 890090 ☺ RG28 7NR

FAIRYTALE FARM | 📍 C3 County

📞 01608 238014 🖥 www.fairytalefarm.co.uk
☺ Fairytale Farm, Southcombe, Chipping Norton, OX7 5QH

Mixing classic fairy tales, animals and adventure play, children will love Fairytale Farm. With their exciting adventure playground, an enchanted walk with a surprise around every corner and a chance to meet their amazing animals, there is so much to see and do. It is a sensory and learning wonderland for all the family.

Race a rubber duck along their pump-powered waterway or see a family of mice going about their daily business in Fairytale Farm's beautifully crafted indoor model village. Where else can you meet mermaids, rabbits, sleeping beauty, alpacas, rheas, sea horses, ducks, chickens and magic?
Adults £7.25 | Children £7

DIDCOT RAILWAY CENTRE | 📍 D5 County

📞 01235 817200 💻 www.didcotrailwaycentre.org.uk

📍 Didcot Parkway Station, Station Road, Didcot, OX11 7NJ

Travel back in time to the golden age of the Great Western Railway. Savour the sights, sounds and smells of steam as you explore this 25-acre living museum with trains dating from Victorian times to the 1960s. Take unlimited rides on steaming days, explore the original 1932 engine shed and see magnificent preserved locomotives - you can even climb onto the footplates of some! See surviving track from Brunel's broad gauge, discover painstakingly restored buildings, carriages and wagons and learn more about the development of railways and how they changed everyday lives.

Open Daily April - September | Weekends October - March | Steam trains running weekends and Wednesdays

OXFORD BUS MUSEUM | 📍 C2 County
MORRIS MOTORS COLLECTION
& HISTORIC CYCLE COLLECTION

📞 01993 883617 💻 www.oxfordbusmuseum.org.uk

📍 Old Station Yard, Main Road, Long Hanborough, Witney, OX29 8LA

200 years of Oxfordshire's road transport is displayed from their 1821 "Dandy horse", an early bicycle, through to their 1881 horse-drawn tram to twentieth century buses, a collection of Morris Motors built in Oxford during Lord Nuffield's era and a historic cycle collection.

They exhibit 35 buses, 20 cars, 50 bicycles, 300 historic photos and numerous old transport artefacts: petrol pumps, road signs, models and ticket machines. The museum has wheelchair friendly walkways, explanatory panels, a viewing gallery where visitors see restorations and running fleet repairs, a cafe, shop and play area.

Wednesdays & Sundays All Year | Saturdays in July & August and most Bank Holidays 10.30am-4.30pm **Adults £5 | Children (ages 5-15) £3 | Under 5's free**

BLETCHLEY PARK | 📍 F2 County

📞 01908 640404 💻 www.bletchleypark.org.uk

📍 Sherwood Drive, Milton Keynes, Buckinghamshire , MK3 6EB

Bletchley Park, once the top-secret home of the World War II Codebreakers, is now a vibrant heritage attraction, open every day to visitors. Step back in time to experience the stories of the extraordinary achievements of the men and women who worked there.

A place of exceptional historical importance, Bletchley Park is also the birthplace of modern computing and has helped shape life as we know it today. Visitor highlights include: restored codebreaking huts, visitor centre, galleries and exhibitions. Discover Bletchley Park's vital D-Day role in a new immersive cinematic experience.

Open Daily March - October: 9.30am - 5pm | November - February: 9.30am - 4pm **Adults £20 | Concessions £17.50 | Children (ages 12-17) £12 | Children under 12 Free**

CHRIST CHURCH | 📍 D5 City

📞 01865 276492   🖥 www.chch.ox.ac.uk
😊 St Aldates, Oxford, OX1 1DP

Walk in the footsteps of academics, kings and queens, Alice in Wonderland and even a few wizards!

Christ Church is open throughout the year. As a working college and cathedral some areas may close from time to time.

For full details on what to see, their opening times, ticket prices, multimedia guide (included in the price of admission), guided tours, services and events visit the Christ Church website. Please note that booking in advance is essential for groups of 10 or more.

OXFORD PHILHARMONIC ORCHESTRA | 📍 Citywide

📞 01865 980980   🖥 www.oxfordphil.com
😊 29A Teignmouth Rd, London, Greater London, NW2 4EB

The Oxford Philharmonic Orchestra present the Oxford Beethoven Festival 2020, a year-long celebration of the composer's 250th anniversary. This includes all his symphonies, concertos, violin, piano & cello sonatas, & his opera Fidelio. Guest artists include Maxim Vengerov, Anne-Sophie Mutter, Jeremy Irons, Martha Argerich, Sir András Schiff, & John Lill. They have a Study Weekend with Alfred Brendel, & Academic Symposium featuring esteemed Beethoven scholars. This goes alongside their ongoing season with concerts featuring the likes of Angela Gheorghiu, & Sir Bryn Terfel, as well as their family concerts 'FUNomusica.'
Box office phone line: Monday - Friday 9am - 6pm

BROUGHTON CASTLE | 📍 C2 County

📞 01295 276070   🖥 www.broughtoncastle.com
😊 Broughton Castle, Banbury, OX15 5EB

Nestled in landscaped gardens and parkland, Broughton Castle is a moated and fortified manor house near Banbury in North Oxfordshire. The grounds include a moat, walled garden with herbaceous borders, where romantic plantings and masses of roses are the highlights. Features include a Medieval Hall, Tudor Ceilings, Civil War connections, ample parking and Tea Room.
The Castle and grounds are open every Sunday, Wednesday and Bank Holiday Monday from April to September. Groups welcome by appointment throughout the year for private visits.
Wednesdays, Sundays & Bank Holiday Mondays | April - September 2pm - 5pm (last admission to Castle 4.30pm)
Adults £10 | Concessions £9 | Children £6 (Gardens only £6)

NEW THEATRE OXFORD | 📍 C3 City

📞 0844 871 3020 🖥 www.atgtickets.com/oxford
📍 George Street, Oxford, OX1 2AG

Playing host to some of the biggest shows and names,
New Theatre Oxford is situated right in the centre of the historic city.

There is always plenty on, from top West End musicals and world
renowned dance companies to the best names in live comedy and
music , there is something to appeal to for everyone.

Box office open Monday – Saturday 12noon – 4pm (box office remains
open until up to 15 minutes after curtain up on performance days) |
Box office phone line open Monday – Sunday 9am – 8pm

CROCODILES OF THE WORLD | 📍 B4 County

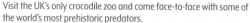

📞 01993 846353 🖥 www.crocodilesoftheworld.co.uk
📍 Burford Road, Brize Norton, OX18 3NX

Visit the UK's only crocodile zoo and come face-to-face with some of
the world's most prehistoric predators.
With talks, feeds and animal encounters throughout the day there's
plenty to keep everyone entertained, including seeing crocodiles being
fed. This fun-filled all-weather attraction is dedicated to crocodile
conservation and home to over 100 crocodiles, including endangered
species, as well as meerkats, giant tortoises and even a komodo
dragon. With keeper experiences, cafe, picnic area, gift shop and
plenty of parking you're guaranteed a wild time.
Open Daily
March - October: 10am - 5pm | November - February: 10am - 4pm

STONEHENGE | 📍 C6 County
| (Further South-West)

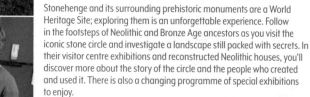

📞 0370 333 1181 🖥 www.english-heritage.org.uk/stonehenge
📍 Stonehenge Visitor Centre, Nr Amesbury, Wiltshire, SP4 7DE

Stonehenge and its surrounding prehistoric monuments are a World
Heritage Site; exploring them is an unforgettable experience. Follow
in the footsteps of Neolithic and Bronze Age ancestors as you visit the
iconic stone circle and investigate a landscape still packed with secrets. In
their visitor centre exhibitions and reconstructed Neolithic houses, you'll
discover more about the story of the circle and the people who created
and used it. There is also a changing programme of special exhibitions
to enjoy.

Open Daily

THE STORY MUSEUM | 📍 D4 City

📞 01865 790050   💻 www.storymuseum.org.uk
📍 The Story Museum, 42 Pembroke Street, Oxford, OX1 1BP

The Story Museum is Oxford's most unusual museum celebrating stories in all forms. Where else could you walk through a wardrobe into Narnia, fly with a snowman or pay a visit to the 100 Acre Wood? The museum has a multitude of spaces where families can lose themselves, including a Whispering Wood, an Enchanted Library and a Treasure Chamber, as well as a packed programme of events including author talks, theatre, music and puppetry in a dedicated performance space, The Shed.
The Story Museum's cafe serves delicious food to suit all ages, so your appetite can have a happy ever after too!
Term Time: Tuesday - Sunday | School Holidays: Open Daily
Monday - Friday: 10am - 5pm | Sunday: 11am - 4pm
Entry from £5. Buy 3 or more tickets to recieve £1 off each ticket

WATERPERRY GARDENS | 📍 E4 County

📞 01844 339226   💻 www.waterperrygardens.co.uk
📍 Waterperry, Near Wheatley, Oxford, OX33 1LA

The 8-acre gardens at Waterperry date back to the 1930's when the estate was home to Beatrix Havergal's famous Ladies Gardening School. It's now one of Oxfordshire's most popular garden attractions, with a quality plant centre and garden shop, gallery, gift barn, museum of rural life and teashop serving homemade lunches and teas.
Waterperry's reputation for education and horticultural excellence continues today with year round arts, crafts and gardening courses and a whole host of annual events. Just a stone's throw from historic Oxford, Waterperry Gardens offer a sense of wellbeing and gardening inspiration.
Open Daily
April - October 10am-5.30pm; November - March 10am-5.00pm

BATSFORD ARBORETUM & GARDEN CENTRE | 📍 B2 County

📞 01386 701441   💻 www.batsarb.co.uk
📍 Batsford, Moreton-in-Marsh, Gloucestershire, GL56 9AD

Batsford is home to one of the country's largest private collections of trees and shrubs. At 56 acres in size, the arboretum is an intimate and romantic place to visit, with interest all year round from the first snowdrops in spring right through to the outstanding autumn colour.
Browse the gift shop and visit the garden centre - a haven for garden and plant lovers. Enjoy delicious lunches, hot drinks and home-baked cakes from the Garden Terrace Café whilst the children burn off some energy in the play area!
Open Daily 9am-5pm Monday - Friday (10am-5pm Sundays & Bank Holidays)
Adults £8.95 | Concessions £7.95 | Children (4-15) £3.50 | Families (2 adults/2 children) £20.00

OXFORD UNITED FOOTBALL CLUB

📍 E6 City (Further South)

📞 01865 337533 💻 www.oufc.co.uk
🙂 Grenoble Road, Oxford, OX4 4XP

Get a real experience of the passion of English football at Oxford United! Easily accessible from the city centre by bus on routes 1, 3a or 5, make sure you take in a game on your visit. Fixtures take place on selected Saturdays (3.00pm) and Tues nights (7.45pm) from August through May. Please visit their website to see whether they have a home match during your visit.

Visitors and families are always welcome to join the 'Yellow Army' at Oxford United home games. Mention it's your first time when booking and their team will make sure you have all the info you need to enjoy the matchday experience. Selected Saturdays and Tuesdays, August - May
From £20 Adults | £11 Under-18s | £7 Under-13s | Under 7s free with an Adult in the Family Area

BLENHEIM PALACE

📍 C3 County

Blenheim Palace is home to the 12th Duke and Duchess of Marlborough and the birthplace of Sir Winston Churchill. Blenheim Palace is a UNESCO World Heritage Site boasting a long and diverse history.
Open daily   10.30am - 5.30pm (last admission 4.45pm)
Adults £27 | Concessions £25 | Children (ages 5-16) £16 | Families (2 adults/2 children) £67.50

💻 www.blenheimpalace.com   📞 01993 810530   🙂 OX20 1UL

COTSWOLD WILDLIFE PARK AND GARDENS | 📍 B4 County

Home to more than 260 species of animals and 120 acres of beautiful parkland. Watch Rhinos graze on the lawns in front of the Gothic Manor House. A fantastic day out for all the family.
Open daily April - October: 10am - 6pm | November - March: 10am - dusk or 5pm
Adults £16 | Concessions £10 | Children (ages 3-16) £10.50

💻 www.cotswoldwildlifepark.co.uk   📞 01993 823 006   🙂 OX18 4JJ

JUNKYARD GOLF CLUB

📍 C4 City

Welcome to Junkyard Golf Club! Home of crazy golf, weird cocktails and all things junk! Get excited on three mashed up 9-hole crazy golf courses created from pre-loved and reclaimed random shizzle.
Open daily 2pm - 12pm Monday - Saturday | 2pm - 10pm Sunday
£8pp Off Peak | £9.50pp Peak

💻 www.junkyardgolfclub.co.uk   🙂 OX1 1PB

OXFORDSHIRE MUSEUM

📍 C3 County

A large 18th century house in the heart of the historic town of Woodstock is home to 11 galleries exploring Oxfordshire's story from the Jurassic period through to Anglo-Saxons and Victorians.
Open daily 10am - 5pm Tuesday - Saturday | 2pm - 5pm Sunday
FREE

💻 www.oxfordshire.gov.uk/museums   📞 01993 814106   🙂 OX20 1SN

WESTGATE OXFORD | 📍 C4 City

Fashion, leisure, restaurants & bars. Westgate Oxford is home to over 100 stores featuring the best of the British high street and prestigious global brands. Visit the roof terrace for restaurants and bars with views over Oxford.

💻 www.westgateoxford.co.uk 📞 01865 263600 ⊗ OX1 1PE

OLIVIA MAY, OXFORD BOUTIQUE | 📍 C1 City

Pop in-store and discover effortless fashion, from wardrobe basics to statement pieces by over 60 international designers across the globe. Fashion shows, styling events and activities by appointment.
Monday - Friday 10am - 5:30pm | Styling Sundays (once per month) 11am - 4pm

💻 www.oliviamay.org 📞 0844 3356323 ⊗ OX1 2HU

VINTAGE DAYS OUT | 📍 Countywide

Vintage Days Out offers private Thames river cruises on Britain's most historic river. · Experiences & Days out · Corporate Entertaining · Wedding Boat & Car Hire

💻 www.vintagedaysout.com 📞 01491 200734 ⊗ Countywide

BICESTER VILLAGE | 📍 D3 County

The ultimate luxury shopping destination, home to more than 160 world-leading brands, from Swarovski to Saint Laurent; all offering exceptional savings. Plus a selection of restaurants and cafés.
Monday - Sunday 9am - 7pm

💻 www.tbvsc.com/bicester-village/en 📞 01869 366266 ⊗ OX26 6WD

ACTIVE ENGLAND TOURS | 📍 Countywide

Active England Tours include cycling and biking, walking, family adventures and multisport tours through beautiful countryside and a host of iconic places.

💻 www.activeenglandtours.com 📞 01865 513007 ⊗ OX4 4GA

COTSWOLD FARM PARK | 📍 B3 County

Adam Henson's Cotswold Farm Park has a long-standing reputation for a fun-filled day out. Visitors of all ages can interact closely with the animals and learn about farming, past and present.

💻 www.cotswoldfarmpark.co.uk 📞 01451 850307 ⊗ GL54 5FL

THE OXFORD ARTISAN DISTILLERY
♀ F3 City (Further East)

📞 01865 767918   🖥 www.spiritoftoad.com
😊 Old Depot, South Park, Cheney Lane, Oxford, OX3 7QJ

Visit TripAdvisor's #1 Thing to Do in Oxford. The Oxford Artisan Distillery is a grain-to-glass distillery that uses locally grown, organic, and exclusive heritage grains to produce a range of award-winning spirits, including gin, absinthe, vodka and whiskey.

The distillery welcomes visitors for friendly, fun and informative tours, offering a unique behind-the-scenes-experience. Tours are a rare opportunity to discover the principles of The Oxford Artisan Distillery approach to distilling, visit the lab and distillery, following the production processes from beginning to end.

Tuesday - Sunday: 11am - 5pm

Tour Operators

CITY SIGHTSEEING OXFORD
♀ Citywide

📞 01865 790522   🖥 www.citysightseeingoxford.com
😊 OX1 1HS

With its medieval streets, cobbled lanes and secluded alleys, there's no better way to see Oxford than up close. Save time and money as you explore on a hop-on, hop-off bus with a loop of 20 stops that's perfect for independent travellers! Enjoy 360-degree views from their top deck and soak up unique stories from their live guides. Audio commentary is available - take your pick from 14 different languages as well as a dedicated kids' commentary. Choose between 24 and 48 hour tickets, or why not select one of their great value combo tickets for discounts on many of Oxford's other top attractions.
Open Daily   9:30am to 5pm | 7 days a week

OXFORD TOUR GUIDES
♀ Citywide

Discover Oxford with qualified Oxford Tour Guides. Choose from general as well as specialist themed tours such as Morse, Lewis and Endeavour or Harry Potter. Tours available in several languages.

🖥 www.oxfordtourguides.co.uk   📞 07769 657145   😊 Based in Oxford

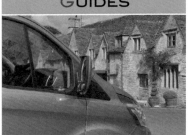

GULLIVER'S GUIDES | 📍 Countywide

📞 07855 141907   🖥 www.gulliversguides.com

😊 Based in Oxford

Oxford · Cotswolds · Stratford · Bath · Stonehenge · Shropshire Hills
Ironbridge · Wye Valley · Windsor and many other places

Tony Gulliver is a qualified Blue Badge Guide with a luxury private-hire minibus. So why not join him on your very own journey of discovery? Combine Oxford with the Cotswolds or Stonehenge with Bath. Tony can mould an itinerary to specific interests such as arts & crafts, great gardens or industrial heritage. For discerning tours with family or friends, go with Gulliver's Guides.

Up to 7 passengers · excellent visibility · air conditioning · live commentary

GO COTSWOLDS | 📍 B2 County

📞 07786 920166   🖥 www.gocotswolds.co.uk   😊 GL56 0AA

Guided small-group day tours of the Cotswolds

Staying in Oxford? Take a day trip out of the city and join Go Cotswolds on a small-group day tour of the Cotswolds Area of Outstanding Natural Beauty! They provide a free pick-up from Moreton-in-Marsh rail station, which has direct rail links to Oxford and London. They can also pick you up and/or drop you off at Leamington Spa and Stratford-upon-Avon rail stations, all accommodation providers in Stratford-upon-Avon, or from Chipping Campden High Street.

In a maximum group size of just 16 people, and with a friendly, local driver-guide, you'll visit seven different locations in the Cotswolds: quaint Chipping Campden, the stunning viewpoint at Dover's Hill, quirky Broadway Tower, bustling Stow-on-the-Wold, beautiful Bibury, and Bourton-on-the-Water - the ever-popular "Venice of the Cotswolds". They also visit their "secret" off-the-beaten-track Cotswolds village - many of their passengers agree that this is the highlight of the tour, but you'll have to join them on a tour to find out!

They're top-rated on TripAdvisor, are "Best Tour Company in the Cotswolds", and have been recommended in several international guide books, including the popular US travel guide "Rick Steves' Great Britain"!
Adults £40 | Children (ages 3-16) £30

COTSWOLD TOURS BY FOWLER TOURS

📍 Countywide

📞 01327 263764   💻 www.fowler-tours.co.uk
😊 Based in Cotswolds

Ken Fowler is an experienced local tour guide with a spacious, air conditioned, VW Sharan which can accommodate small groups of up to six adults. Tours include a private home and garden visit, full day tours, short day tours (6 hours), winter short day tours and longer tours of the United Kingdom.

Discover hidden villages, churches and historical sites amongst the honey-coloured limestone and rolling hills of the beautiful Cotswolds. His tour guiding service is flexible and routes can be tailored to your interests and include specific attractions. To check availability please contact Ken.

CONCIERGE HISTORY TOURS

📍 Countywide

📞 07714 765696   💻 www.conciergehistorytours.co.uk

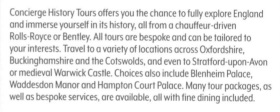

Concierge History Tours offers you the chance to fully explore England and immerse yourself in its history, all from a chauffeur-driven Rolls-Royce or Bentley. All tours are bespoke and can be tailored to your interests. Travel to a variety of locations across Oxfordshire, Buckinghamshire and the Cotswolds, and even to Stratford-upon-Avon or medieval Warwick Castle. Choices also include Blenheim Palace, Waddesdon Manor and Hampton Court Palace. Many tour packages, as well as bespoke services, are available, all with fine dining included.

Please see website for more detailed information.

OMC GLOBAL

📍 Countywide

📞 01865 3777775   💻 www.omcglobal.co.uk

OMC Provides luxury Transport from 7-36 seater with the following services:

- Europe & UK Tours
- Day Trips
- Airport Transfers
- Weddings
- Corporate Events
- Sports Events
- Blue Badge Guides

24 hour service

Where to Eat & Drink

103

CHERWELL BOATHOUSE

📍 C1 City
(Further North)

📞 01865 552746 🖥 www.cherwellboathouse.co.uk
📍 Bardwell Road, Oxford, OX2 6ST

The Cherwell Boathouse is an iconic Oxford punt station and restaurant on the banks of the river Cherwell close to the centre of Oxford. The restaurant serves seasonal modern English food, with an award-winning wine list and friendly service throughout the year.

Both the restaurant and Marquee overlooking the river are wonderful places to celebrate all types of occasion. They can cater for corporate days out, functions and parties with conference facilities and option of punting alongside .

Restaurant Open All Year | Punting Open Mid March - Mid October
Restaurant Lunch: 12-2.30pm | Restaurant Dinner: 6pm-9.30pm | Punting 10am - dusk

FORMOSAN TEA BAR - AUTHENTIC BUBBLE TEA & KOMBUCHA ON TAP

📍 D4 City

📞 01865 200911 🖥 www.formosan.co.uk
📍 128A High Street, Oxford, OX1 4DF

The only tea bar of its kind in the UK, pioneering healthy bubble tea since 2012. Tea leaves from world best tea-farming regions of Taiwan selected by Formosan tea master. Only natural high quality ingredients used to make their bubble teas. The nation's only Kombucha 'on tap' served in the shop. Every cup of tea expertly made to perfection. They are a local independent business and they care. Free samples available to help you find your favourite in no time.
享受無負擔的茶香美味, 盡在牛津福爾摩沙。
台灣老闆直營, 品質保證! 健康、天然、無負擔！
80年代的本場台湾バブルティーをあなたのもとへ
タピオカ ミルクティー、バブル レモングリーンティー
Open Daily Monday - Friday: 11am - 7pm | Saturday: 10am - 7pm | Sunday: 11am - 6pm

PHO

📍 C5 City

Find Pho on the top of the Westgate shopping centre, where they serve their healthy Vietnamese food all day every day. Stop in to enjoy noodles, pho, salads and much more beside.
Sunday - Tuesday: 11:30am - 9:30pm, Wednesday - Friday: 11:30am - 10pm, Saturday: 11:30am - 10:30pm

🖥 www.phocafe.co.uk/locations/oxford   📞 01865 980 209   📍 OX1 1PG

104

THE ALCHEMIST WESTGATE OXFORD | 📍 C5 City

📞 01865 792072   ☺ Westgate Roof Terrace, Oxford, OX1 1TR
🖥 www.thealchemist.uk.com/venues/oxford-westgate-centre

Located on the rooftop of the Westgate centre in Oxford, The Alchemist really has the best views around. Enjoy spectacular cocktails and glorious food on their wrap around terrace. The Alchemist are masters in the dark arts of molecular mixology and demons in the kitchen. Their mixologists create every cocktail with an obsessive eye for detail, presented in vessels orchestrated to add a devilish dash of theatre - they bedazzle, bewitch and set the scene for everything they do. Enjoy flaming cocktails and delicious all-day dining that's become the Alchemist trademark - Theatre Served.

Open Daily Monday - Thursday: 10am - 12am | Friday: 10am - 1am |
Saturday: 10am - 2am | Sunday: 10am - 11pm

OXFORD CASTLE QUARTER | 📍 C4 City

The Oxford Castle Quarter blends past and present, making every visit a memorable experience. Discover great places to eat and drink, historic attractions and a unique atmospheric hotel.
Monday - Sunday: 6:00am - 11:30pm | Please check individual business opening hours

🖥 www.oxfordcastlequarter.com/   📞 01865 201657   ☺ OX1 1AY

THE YURT CAFÉ AT NICHOLSONS	01869 340342	www.nicholsonsgb.com/retail/yurt-cafe	OX25 6HL	📍 D3 County
QUOD	01865 202505	www.quod.co.uk	OX1 4BJ	📍 E4 City
KEEPERS KITCHEN & BAR	01865 248695	www.keeperskitchenandbar.co.uk/keepers-oxford	OX1 4BE	📍 F4 City
GEE'S RESTAURANT & BAR	01865 553540	www.geesrestaurant.co.uk	OX2 6PE	📍 C1 City (Further North)
THE COCONUT TREE OXFORD	01865 421865	www.thecoconut-tree.com/oxford	OX4 1AH	📍 F4 City (Further East)
SWOON	01865 411677	www.swoononaspoon.co.uk	OX1 4AH	📍 D4 City
GIGGLING SQUID	01865 557696	www.gigglingsquid.com/restaurant/oxford	OX2 6AE	📍 B1 City
CINNAMON KITCHEN OXFORD	01865 951670	www.cinnamon-kitchen.com/westgate-oxford	OX1 1TR	📍 C4 City
SHORYU RAMEN OXFORD	shoryu.oxford@shoryuramen.com	www.shoryuramen.com/stores/82	OX1 1PB	📍 C4 City
THE LION AT WENDLEBURY	01869 388228	www.thelionwendlebury.co.uk	OX25 2PW	📍 D3 County
PARSONAGE GRILL	01865 292305	www.parsonagegrill.co.uk	OX2 6NN	📍 C1 City
CAFE LOCO	01865 200959	www.goingloco.com	OX1 1RA	📍 D4 City